Essays and Studies 2009

Series Editor: Peter Kitson

The English Association

The objects of the English Association are to promote the knowledge and appreciation of the English language and its literature, and to foster good practice in its teaching and learning at all levels.

The Association pursues these aims by creating opportunities of co-operation among all those interested in English; by furthering the recognition of English as essential in education; by discussing methods of English teaching; by holding lectures, conferences, and other meetings; by publishing journals, books, and leaflets; and by forming local branches.

Publications

The Year's Work in English Studies. An annual bibliography. Published by Blackwell.

The Year's Work in Critical and Cultural Theory. An annual bibliography. Published by Blackwell.

Essays and Studies. An annual volume of essays by various scholars assembled by the collector covering usually a wide range of subjects and authors from the medieval to the modern. Published by D.S. Brewer.

English. A journal of the Association, *English* is published three times a year by the Association.

The Use of English. A journal of the Association, *The Use of English* is published three times a year by the Association.

Newsletter. A *Newsletter* is published three times a year giving information about forthcoming publications, conferences, and other matters of interest.

Benefits of Membership

Institutional Membership

Full members receive copies of *The Year's Work in English Studies*, *Essays and Studies*, *English* (3 issues) and three *Newsletters*.

Ordinary Membership covers *English* (3 issues) and three *Newsletters*.

Schools Membership includes copies of each issue of *English* and *The Use of English*, one copy of *Essays and Studies*, three *Newsletters*, and preferential booking and rates for various conferences held by the Association.

Individual Membership

Individuals take out Basic Membership, which entitles them to buy all regular publications of the English Association at a discounted price, and attend Association gatherings.

For further details write to The Secretary, The English Association, The University of Leicester, University Road, Leicester, LE1 7RH.

Essays and Studies 2009

Authors at Work
The Creative Environment

Edited by
Ceri Sullivan and Graeme Harper

for the English Association

D. S. BREWER

ESSAYS AND STUDIES 2009
IS VOLUME SIXTY-TWO IN THE NEW SERIES
OF ESSAYS AND STUDIES COLLECTED ON BEHALF OF
THE ENGLISH ASSOCIATION
ISSN 0071–1357

First published 2009
D. S. Brewer, Cambridge

D. S. Brewer is an imprint of Boydell & Brewer Ltd
PO Box 9, Woodbridge, Suffolk IP12 3DF, UK
and of Boydell & Brewer Inc.
668 Mt Hope Avenue, Rochester, NY 14620, USA
website: www.boydellandbrewer.com

ISBN 978–1–84384–195–1

A CIP catalogue record for this title is available
from the British Library

The Library of Congress has cataloged this serial publication:
Catalog card number 36–8431

This publication is printed on acid-free paper

Printed in Great Britain by
CPI Antony Rowe, Chippenham and Eastbourne

Contents

LIST OF ILLUSTRATIONS   vii

ACKNOWLEDGEMENTS   ix

NOTES ON CONTRIBUTORS AND INTERVIEWEES   x

INTRODUCTION   1
Ceri Sullivan

GUBBINS AT A DESK: AUDEN'S CAVE   21
Stan Smith

LITERARY LIMELIGHT: THE LAUREATESHIP   39
Interview: Andrew Motion

A BED OF ONE'S OWN: MARGARET OLIPHANT   49
Elisabeth Jay

LITERARY ARCHIVES: THE BRITISH LIBRARY   69
Interview: Jamie Andrews

GLUE AND DAYDREAMS: TROLLOPE AT WORK   79
N. John Hall

LITERARY NETSCAPES: WEB POETRY AND BLOGGING   101
Interview: Robert Sheppard

GROWING UP AND ZONING OUT: CHARLOTTE   107
    AND EMILY BRONTË
Stevie Davies

LITERARY FESTIVALS: HAY-ON-WYE   125
Interview: Peter Florence

COMPOSING PARADISE LOST: BLINDNESS   129
    AND THE FEMININE
Peter C. Herman

LITERARY HERITAGE: STRATFORD AND THE GLOBE   147
Conversation: Farah Karim-Cooper and Kate Rumbold

TAVERN AND LIBRARY: WORKING WITH BEN JONSON   155
Michelle O'Callaghan and *Adam Smyth*

POSTSCRIPT   173
Graeme Harper

INDEX   179

List of Illustrations

Plate 1: Margaret Oliphant's drawing-room and study in Windsor.   54
Photograph by Maurice Lévy in the possession of the author.

Plate 2: Manuscript page from Anthony Trollope's   82
Mr. Scarborough's Family (the beginning of Chapter 22, written
in June 1881). Robert H. Taylor Collections. Department of Rare
Books and Special Collections, Princeton University Library.

Plate 3: Trollope's working diary for Framley Parsonage,   86
1 November 1859 to 9 April 1860. MS. Don. C9 Sadleir
Collection, Bodleian Library, University of Oxford.

Plate 4: Arthur Dixon, 'Blind Milton Dictating his Immortal   132
Poem', in Newnes' Pictorial Book of Knowledge, ed. H. A. Pollock
(London: the Home Book Company). Bridgeman Art Gallery.
Undated copy in private hands.

Plate 5: Mihaly Munkacsy, 'Blind Milton Dictating Paradise   136
Lost to his Daughters,' 1878. Collections of the New York Public
Library, Astor, Lenox, and Tilden Foundations.

Acknowledgements

The editors would like to thank Stephen Colclough, Ian Gregson, Peter Kitson, Clare McManus, Andrew Moor, and Samantha Rayner for their suggestions and for reading some of the material. We are grateful to Helen Lucas of the English Association for her incisive dealings with the publisher, contracts, and permissions. Thanks also to Linda Jones of Bangor University for help with the copy-editing and the team at Boydell & Brewer. They worked with speed, efficiency, and courtesy.

Ceri Sullivan is responsible for the primary editing, the conversation, and the introduction, Graeme Harper the interviews and postscript.

Notes on Contributors and Interviewees

Jamie Andrews   is Head of Modern Literary Manuscripts at the British Library and a member of the UK Literary Heritage Working Group.

Stevie Davies   is a Fellow of the Royal Society of Literature, Fellow of the Welsh Academy and Director of Creative Writing at Swansea University. She is a literary critic, historian, and novelist. Her novels have been long-listed for the Booker and Orange Prizes; *The Element of Water* won the Arts Council of Wales Book of the Year award for 2002. Stevie is the author of four books on Emily Bronte; she has edited *The Tenant of Wildfell Hall* and *Jane Eyre* for Penguin Classics. Her latest novel is *The Eyrie* (Weidenfeld & Nicolson, 2007).

Peter Florence   is Director of the biggest literary festival in the world, the Hay Festival, started in 1988, rumoured to be with winnings from a poker game.

N. John Hall   is Distinguished Professor of English at Bronx Community College and the Graduate Center, City University of New York. Among his publications are *The Letters of Anthony Trollope* (Stanford University Press, 1983), *Trollope: A Biography* (Clarendon Press, 1991), *Max Beerbohm Caricatures* (Yale University Press, 1997), *Max Beerbohm: A Kind of a Life* (Yale University Press, 2002), and *Belief: A Memoir* (Frederic C. Beil, 2007).

Graeme Harper   is Professor of Creative Writing at Bangor University. He has recently published *The Creative Writing Guidebook* (Continuum, 2008) and *Creative Writing Studies: Practice, Research, Pedagogy* (MLM, 2008) with J. Kroll. He is currently working on *Creative Writing? On a Philosophy of Creative Text* and a new novel, *Camera Phone*, for publication in 2009.

Peter C. Herman   is Professor of English and Comparative Literature at San Diego State University. He is the author of *Destabilizing Milton: 'Paradise Lost' and the Poetics of Incertitude* (Palgrave, 2005) and the editor of *Approaches to Teaching Milton's Shorter Poetry and Prose* (MLA, 2007). His current project is *'Royal Poetrie': Monarchic Verse* *and the Early Modern Political Imaginary* (Cornell University Press, forthcoming).

Elisabeth Jay is Professor of English, Director of the Institute for Historical and Cultural Research, and Associate Dean of Arts and Humanities at Oxford Brookes University. Her publications include a literary biography of Margaret Oliphant, as well as editions of autobiographies, biographies, and fiction by a number of Victorian women writers, together with a range of work on nineteenth-century literature and theology.

Farah Karim-Cooper is Head of Courses and Research, Globe Education and Research Fellow, King's College London. She chairs the Globe Architecture Research Group and sits on advisory boards for various theatre projects. Her publications include *Cosmetics in Shakespearean and Renaissance Drama* (Edinburgh University Press, 2006) and *Shakespeare's Globe: A Theatrical Experiment* (Cambridge University Press, 2008), co-edited with Christie Carson.

Andrew Motion is Great Britain's Poet Laureate and Professor of Creative Writing at Royal Holloway College, London. His new collection is *The Cinder Path* (Faber, 2009)

Michelle O'Callaghan is a Reader at the University of Reading. She is the author of *The English Wits: Literature and Sociability in Early Modern England* (Cambridge University Press, 2007), *The 'Shepheards Nation': Jacobean Spenserians and early Stuart political culture* (Oxford University Press, 2000), and *Thomas Middleton, Renaissance Dramatist* (Edinburgh University Press, forthcoming 2009).

Kate Rumbold is Post-doctoral Research Fellow at the Shakespeare Institute, Stratford-upon-Avon. She co-ordinates the major AHRC-funded project 'Interrogating Cultural Value in the Twenty-First Century: the Case of Shakespeare', and is writing a book on that topic with Kate McLuskie. She has published articles on twenty-first and eighteenth-century Shakespeare, and is completing a monograph on Shakespeare in the eighteenth-century novel.

Robert Sheppard is Professor of Creative Writing at Edge Hill University. He runs a poetry zine on www.robertsheppard.blogspot.

com. His most recent book is *The Poetry of Saying: British Poetry and its Discontents 1905–2000* (Liverpool University Press, 2006).

Stan Smith is Research Professor in Literary Studies at Nottingham Trent University. He has published eight books on modern literature, including two on W. H. Auden. He edited the English Association's centenary volume of *Essays and Studies* on *Globalisation and its Discontents* (2006). A first collection of poems, *Family Fortunes*, was published in 2008 (Shoestring Press). He is series editor of Longman Critical Readers, Longman Studies in Twentieth-Century Literature, and Irish Academic Press's new series, *Visions and Revisions: Irish Writers in their Time*, which includes his own volume on Patrick Kavanagh.

Adam Smyth is a Lecturer in English at the University of Reading. He has written *'Profit and Delight': Printed Miscellanies in England, 1640–1682* (Wayne State University Press, 2004), and edited *Drink and Conviviality in Seventeenth-Century England* (D. S. Brewer, 2004). He is currently completing a new monograph entitled *Life-Writing in Early Modern England*.

Ceri Sullivan is Reader in English at Bangor University. Her latest book is *The Rhetoric of the Conscience in Donne, Herbert, and Vaughan* (Oxford University Press, 2008); her other books deal with rhetoric in Catholic prose, fantasy, and credit in mercantile writing. She is halfway through a monograph on how John Milton, Anthony Trollope, and David Hare find a creative element in administrative work.

Introduction

CERI SULLIVAN

THE IMAGE of the creative artist was once of someone who rose above his circumstances. Indeed, their biographers often dwelt fondly on situations the rest of us might find dispiriting or distracting, from garrets to boot-blacking factories. These Pollyannas showed how the writer could draw the metaphysical out of the physical (though the latter could return, of course, as material or copy). The mind, it was declared, rather grandly, was its own place.

Postmodern geography, however, heralds a transcendence of the old stabilities of place. Modern communications, particularly those that are televisual or involve the internet, allow a writer to be in multiple places as he writes, to choose the places in which the mind 'is.' The emphasis thus shifts from transcending the environment, finding the source of inspiration within, to co-operating with or even controlling the environment. The newest branches of literary criticism reverberate to the reworking of 'real' place, from publishing history to ecocriticism. Where earlier scholars looked at the psychology of the creative artist when imagination swept over him, this collection takes up research into creativity to recognize context and reception. In material terms, process and output are of as much interest as producer.

The effect on a range of institutions is startling. City planners develop flexible and diverse spaces to attract creative people. Government policy and grants flow into the knowledge economy. The creative industries sector turns out to generate cash not consume subsidies. Business embeds training in innovation into leadership programmes. Libraries wonder what, apart from manuscripts, they should archive from an artist's estate, and make judgements regarding the value and importance of what was once considered writerly ephemera. Heritage bodies market pilgrimages to places where Literature flourished. Schools, colleges, and universities are urged to act as talent magnets, educating intellectual entrepreneurs, marrying creativity and employability.

The notion that if we get our human environment right we will all be more creative is a heart-warming one. Is it true? This collection is the first to take up this idea from three alternate points of view: poets, critics, and literary 'industrialists' from the British Library, the Hay-on-Wye Literary Festival, Stratford-on-Avon, and the Globe. They ask how imaginative texts can be set alongside evidence of a specific writer's environment, to reveal more of the creative process. Accordingly, the introduction will start from the widest perspective, by looking at theories of creativity, then narrow down to look at the environments demanded by the creative industries, before finally focusing on what writers have said about their own working methods.

The Psychology of Creativity

The figure of the solitary genius had already lost its grip by the middle of the twentieth century, in part due to the influence of research by Graham Wallas. He systematized reflections by the French mathematician Henri Poincaré on his breakthrough moments. Poincaré's account is legendary.

> For fifteen days … I seated myself at my work table, stayed an hour or two, tried a great number of combinations and reached no results. One evening, contrary to my custom, I drank black coffee and could not sleep. Ideas rose in crowds; I felt them collide until pairs interlocked, so to speak, making a stable combination. By the next morning I had established the existence of a class of [mathematical] functions. (Ghiselin 1952, 25)

Wallas pointed out that Poincaré reports a four-stage experience. First comes preparation, where the creator works over and over previous research in the same area, endlessly turning the problem to and fro in his mind, a time of hard, conscious, systematic – and fruitless – endeavour. When he becomes exhausted, he puts the work aside in favour of very different activities, moving discipline, or medium, or area. Wallas called this the incubation period, where ideas and experiences are left to float without purpose, drifting against each other, forming and reforming new patterns and associations. Then comes the traditional moment of inspiration, where a new pattern flashes into the mind as correct, as the solution to the formal problem dwelt on for so long. Finally, such a pattern is evaluated and verified, using traditional methods of research.

There are two consequences of using this model. When inspiration is joined to preparation and incubation, creativity can be questioned in terms of context by both government and scholars. Can pedagogues and town councils alike come up with places that allow formal, purposeful investigation at one time and, at another, playful diversity? At the end of the process, when inspiration is joined by verification, creativity can be questioned in terms of its output. Is the idea new itself? Is it significant? Can it be reproduced? Such a stress on product rather than artist lies behind the business world's decision to use 'innovative' (not 'creative') as the adjective to praise new and profitable forms of work. The move from producer to environment and output began with Wallas's ideas.

Other research into creativity tended to prove that Wallas's model was robust. Psychoanalysts had already recognized the links between creativity and incubation. Sigmund Freud and D. W. Winnicott both pointed to the safe unreality of play as a space where tangible objects can be linked to wishes and successfully manipulated (Freud 1959; Winnicott 1971). Play, Winnicott observed, occurs in the mid-location between the inner reality of the individual and the shared reality of an external world. It is a non-purposive activity that allows the creator of the fictions to meditate in safety on problems or unfulfilled desires. Creative writers, Freud postulated, allow other people access to their phantasy objects in language.

From Freud and Winnicott's perspective, the young (or those otherwise outside professional or disciplinary boxes) are peculiarly able to conceive of new conceptual space, and change the generative rules informing their ideas. However, certain disciplines are specifically structured to enable the movement from formal research to formless and unmotivated play and back. There is a tantalizing possibility that literary criticism and creative writing are keys to this more wide-spread creativity, which is demonstrably useful to society and the economy. Wallas considered that preparatory thinking activates relevant ideas in the unconscious, which then selects a few to bring together, either randomly or by their aesthetic qualities. Literature is an 'institution' which is peculiarly expert in the area of incubation, bi-sociating ideas through analogies, verbal play, and dramatic structures. This delicately sociable conceptual system demands a good memory, a store of past patterns and ideas to muse over. It also requires a personality which is able to 'make do' with probabilities rather than certainties, and enjoys living at the edge of concepts and disciplines. Such an activity is essentially and necessarily led by synchronicities. Will belongs to the conscious life only. It is effective in attaining objects in view, but it cannot enable us to move in directions that have not yet been discovered. To select a subject against inclination and force the mind to elaborate it is both damaging and diminishing (Ghiselin 1952, 17).

Where Freud and Winnicott saw childish defences and desires,

Abraham Maslow in the 1960s saw adult self-actualization. The ability to hold disparate or even seemingly contradictory levels of meaning in mind at one time requires people who are able to see

> the fresh, the raw, the concrete, the ideographic, as well as the generic, the abstract, the rubicised, the categorised, and the classified. Consequently, they live far more in the real world of nature than in the verbalised world of concepts, abstractions, expectations, beliefs, and stereotypes that most people confuse with the real world.
> (Maslow 1976, 90)

The exceptional artist has the courage to accept that reality may not be as we think. Relatively unfrightened by stepping out of line, she works without self-censorship and is attracted to mysteries, new ideas, problems – to the boundaries of the discipline. She can be, 'when the total objective situation calls for it, comfortably disorderly, sloppy, anarchic, chaotic, vague, doubtful, uncertain, indefinite, approximate, inexact, or inaccurate' (Maslow 1976, 87). Note the reservation: when the total situation calls for it. The creator who engages with multiple ideas and stimuli at once in a messy or playful way is also the same person who has spent many disciplined hours studying previous work in the area, and will go on to audit the results of his play, with a fierce regard for standards. Willpower, discipline, and effort matter in the first and last stages of creativity, what Katherine Mansfield called terrific hard gardening.

The Creative Environment

The ideal creative environment, then, allows focused research and relaxed, diverse experiences. Richard Florida and Charles Landry were among the first to think this through in terms of city planning (Florida 2002; Landry 2000). Creativity, they proclaimed, is now the decisive source of competitive advantage for companies. Rather than signing up for life with one employer, temporary workers in the knowledge economy bring well-developed skills to specific problems in a number of companies. This 'portfolio' career structure needs the employee to move flexibly from project to project. The company must maintain a social infrastructure which encourages a reservoir of talent. Thus creatives congregate in certain spaces so they can move projects with ease, and companies locate there to select qualified personnel for each project. Geography has become the matrix that matches people and jobs, not because the tasks themselves require physical proximity but because the creative environment requires it.

Such employees define themselves more by what they are doing at work than by traditional social identities. The presence of family and friends may interfere with thinking through an idea more than the weaker claims of acquaintanceship. Thus, the anonymity found in cities is particularly helpful to allow many but weak social ties to develop. The worker takes his cue from the exigencies of the project rather than a timesheet. Hours of concentration are followed by hours of musing, and the context has to allow this, with workspaces to think in, but also places to dawdle, to look around, to have a coffee, to meet different people. A cultural infrastructure that promotes public discussion, events, and exhibitions is needed. In such a utopia the workplace is everywhere, controlled rather by peer evaluation and self-motivation than managerial supervision. Losing the strict demarcation between home and work, this workplace is both more stressful and more caring. It is brutally stressful to be constantly creative, and at the same time the smart firm, the smart city, gives its workers what they need to be creative. As Florida concludes, insisting on this sort of rich space is not self-indulgence but an economically rational way of behaving. We live by our creativity, so we take care of it and seek environments that allow it to flourish (Florida 2002, 132 ff, 192 ff).

Though Florida and Landry cover all forms of the knowledge economy, their views are particularly relevant to the 'creative industries': the high arts, craft, performance, fashion, design, advertising, and multimedia. Since the late 1990s, between 6 and 8 per cent of employment in the larger cities in the UK has been in this sector, which is growing at twice the rate of the economy as a whole. These industries are populated by people in their twenties and thirties, who exploit their intangible personal assets, such as ingenuity and imagination, just as much as they do their technical skills. They prize autonomy, are entrepreneurial, and do not feel threatened by technology. Taken on to solve a particular problem or test a particular boundary, e-lancers are used to job insecurity. To cope with the risk, they develop wide networks of contacts and a range of skills to sell on. Reputation matters when the next employer could be the current customer, so creatives have a strong work ethic, a drive to complete jobs on time to the highest possible standard.

Centred on well-developed and unique visions, firms in the creative industries tend to be small, and to work within an ecology of peers rather than in a linear supply chain. They often take care of the whole process, from initial concept and design to production and distribution. Sometimes, production and retailing may be handed over to larger companies or agents. Their size encourages multi-tasking, since people must improvise and cross roles. Creative firms which get larger and source their project teams from within themselves have to combat a growing familiarity between team members as well as creeping over-specialization by each employee, where the retreat into habitual tasks stops any creative cross-over (Hartley 2005). Since each product in the creative world is unique, reception by knowledgeable critics is important. The A list/B list phenomenon of the art world develops, where audiences, critics, and investors eye up each other's reactions, until the positive feed-back loop, the buzz, is picked up by a cool-hunting, larger-scale distributor (Bilton 2007, 103).

This demonstrates no necessary chasm between creative artist and environment manager. Indeed, firms acknowledge that simply leaving the former alone can produce 'the paralysis of too many possibilities … The expectation of an effortless, spontaneous release of pure inventiveness is a burden rather than a gift.' Even individual artists, therefore, impose their own rules to produce a bounded conceptual space within which experiment takes place. External constraints such as physical resources provide focal points around which to organize random impulses. 'Deadline magic' occurs, where just-in-time decisions are made because they have to be, there and then. Creative solutions habitually happen up against the wire, where inventiveness and decisiveness are needed (Bilton 2007, 72–85). There has, of course, long been recognition that the art market is one where producers, evaluators, and consumers make economically rational decisions. The medieval ecclesiastical artist and the contemporary video-installation artist ask the same questions: what medium to work in, where to site production, which parts can be farmed out and which done in-house, how to advertise, whose endorsements to seek, how to price the work, how many copies to produce, and so on (Caves 2000, 2–68). The creative world has always involved managing the work environment.

Conversely, managers – even those outside the creative industries – are turning to creativity theory (Amabile 1996; Henry 2006). Companies such as Standard Chartered Bank claim creativity as a core value. Business degrees and MBAs now habitually run modules developing employee creativity. Even railway bookstores have shelves of self-help books by management gurus, each pressing innovation onto passing executives. The Open University's postgraduate module on Creativity, Innovation, and Change (B822) is a useful example of this sort of education. The module is structured around three blocks. The first is psychological, asking the student to investigate how perception, style, and culture affect creativity, and to think about a personality inventory. The second is technical, where the student acquires a portfolio of tools to explore problems, generate ideas, make decisions, get co-workers to agree them, and plan to put them into action. The third is organizational, thinking through the actions needed to re-engineer a company's culture, internally and externally, such as scanning the environment in which it works and scenario planning. Throughout, the module stresses that creativity tends to arise in corporate situations where there is safety, freedom to explore ideas, and a climate open to diversity. Moreover, it requires its students to employ what has been learned in their own companies; they must test their conclusions against reality.

Though colleagues in English – more used to an organic approach – may be dismayed at the precision with which a library of over 150 mental tools is offered, they may also find something exhilarating in the way a topic or problem is turned round and round (uncannily like a creative writing exercise). It takes imagination, tacit knowledge, persuasive force, emotional energy, and a strong will to take a sideways look at the present, hear intimations of what does not yet exist, write the script, staff this with virtual characters, and then turn it from virtual reality to hard fact. Reflecting on his experiences in the creative department of an advertising agency, one manager noted how 'heat and passion and inflammation and abrasion' are essential; 'often the brilliant breakthrough is achieved by the bloody-minded will of one person' (John Sparrow, in Henry 2006, 85).

As business takes this linguistic turn, there are openings for literary experts, exploited by companies such as Richard Olivier's Mythodrama. Olivier sells day-long 'experiences' where Shakespeare's plays are recast by top executives to solve corporate problems (the BBC, Nokia, Shell, and the like have used *Macbeth* and *Julius Caesar* to deal with appropriate ambition and boardroom conflict). There are even grant schemes for academics to work with companies by offering their ability to analyse representations and inspire creativity, such the Knowledge Transfer schemes run by the Arts and Humanities Research Council. One recent scheme used research into the way the medieval Catholic Inquisition investigated communication between heretics to show a management consultancy how to train its clients in bottom-up networking. Intelligence is not only or even essentially rational; as the CEO of a publishing giant said of business schools, 'they train their students to sound wonderful. But it's necessary to find out if there's any *judgement* behind their language' (cited by Guy Claxton, in Henry 2006, 47). Cue English, the only discipline which is expert in creating detailed and substantive thought experiments into the 'what ifs.'

Thus there are social, political, and economic reasons why government wonks, think-tanks, and funders alike should be interested in supporting a creative environment for all. However, some commentators are less gung-ho about the notion. As Bilton says, the older myth that creativity is a form of untaught genius is helpful for the Treasury: no training needed, and a rationale which satisfies those working at the bottom of the creative industries, in temporary and voluntary roles. Even where action is taken in good faith to support these industries it tends to be ham-fisted. Government departments working with job creation are used to dealing with large inward investment in single companies to create thousands of jobs, not with small amounts of support to thousands of tiny companies to create a single job in each. Business advisers lack the knowledge, time, and interest to handle micro-enterprises (whose staff respond best to informal and tailored skills transfer), and venture capital is only available on the large scale.

James Heartfield is even less optimistic. In a situation of declining natural resources and community breakdown, the creative industries promised the government cheap employment and social and physical regeneration. Heartfield thinks it nonsense to suppose that Britain can compensate for long-term, large-scale industrial decline by living on its wits (Heartfield 2000). Indeed, the Department of Trade and Industry report which dubbed Britain a knowledge economy was preceded by an internal memorandum saying that there were few other economic ideas around. The things that used to be called wrong about the old economy are cited as good about the new: a large service sector (servicing the time-poor, cash-rich knowledge workers), job insecurity (now called flexibility), and youth unemployment (now called expanding higher education). Heartfield concludes that the popular use of the creative industries to explain the state of Britain's economy refers simply to an aspiration to escape from the burgeoning number of uncreative service sector jobs.

The Literary Angle

Fantasy or reality, the widespread and often passionate belief in creativity-for-all has put libraries, archives, heritage organizations, and educational institutions on their mettle. Literary repositories, from archives to heritage properties, are grappling with the idea of how to demonstrate the specific creativity of the environments they are charged with conserving. Even selecting what constitutes evidence of this environment is problematic. The UK Group for Literary Manuscripts and Archives (GLAM), for instance, naturally lists as its concern literary manuscripts from all phases of composition (preparation, in the form of notes, sketches, drawings, marginalia, through the composition phase, with drafts, reworkings, fair copies, proofs, editors' proofs, to post-publication annotations by the author). Yet it also considers that other personal documents relating to the writer throw light on the composition of the text: letters (friends and family, business, financial, cultural), reviews, audio-visual material, e-records, cuttings, legal documents, and even objects such as typewriters and pens. Then come the issues of copyright and data protection. In the case of the latter, for instance, literary papers typically contain much sensitive personal data, which means every document must be read before being issued to a researcher. This can conflict with the principle of freedom of information; determining what might cause substantial damage and distress to a particular individual is a subjective and unpredictable process. Moreover, since writers often choose to make their private lives public in their creative writing, and often socialize with colleagues and competitors in the writing world, any distinction between public work and private life is blurred.

Two poets have approached this problem, one as a professional librarian, the other as poet laureate. Philip Larkin defined the remit of the literary archive as 'anything that makes up the archive of a creative writer's life and constitutes the background of his works.' He urged libraries to take a bet on current authors, to initiate collections and not wait until a writer had proved famous. The reader, he thought, approached such manuscripts in meaningful terms and also in magical ways: 'this is the paper [the author] wrote on, these are the words as he wrote them, emerging for the first time in this particular miraculous combination' (Larkin 1979, 34). Larkin's biographer Andrew Motion, speaking at the British Library in 2006, also looked for the emerging sense of 'planning and plotting and scheming and timing' in the engine room of the poem, in manuscripts that show how inspiration and craftsmanship coalesce, moment by moment. How then to catch the diverse and voluminous forms of text from the digital age, the emails, hypertexts, blogs, e-books, websites, videos, podcasts, and memory sticks? And this list will be out of date before this book leaves the press.

Drawing the boundary is also difficult because there is no uniformity to the physical, financial, and social circumstances which writers find necessary to the work in hand. The element of creativity that involves conscious work is more easily separated out, conserved, and displayed: the writer's library, his drafts, and so on. But what about the many and diverse other contexts that are part of the act of writing? Clare composed as he rambled, noting down words in his hat rim if he needed to; Wesley wrote his hymns to the rhythm of his horse, trotting between sermon engagements with his travelling desk; Donne was dismally prompted to write his most witty poems when surrounded by wet nappies; Johnson heeded the printer's devil knocking at his door; de Quincey took opium; Dickens stood at a clerk's desk for hours. The heritage industry is feeling its way towards capturing this range of experience, attempting to embody the magic which Larkin talked about. As actors know, putting oneself into the position of another produces bodily connections that affect how one acts: a bodily stance affects the mind. The hunger for literary anecdotes, from formal biographies to literary festivals, shows a wistful sense of wanting to make the magic ourselves. Here, digital technology helps separate the meaning from the magic. It is relatively easy to programme a virtual scriptorium, pulling together manipulable images of the habitat of the writer even though its objects are scattered. Yet the desire to look at the things themselves is still strong, though one may only see a fraction of their number. Hence the long and continuing history of forgery, though facsimile is so easy (and legal) to produce.

Educational institutions are still mulling over whether it is possible to teach creativity. In his inaugural lecture as Professor of Poetry at Oxford in 1956, Auden teased his audience with his fantasy of a college for bards. Four languages would be studied (English, one ancient, two modern), thousands of lines of poetry learned by heart, the only critical exercise required would be parody, and there would be two sets of courses, one in prosody, rhetoric, and philology, the other in mathematics, natural history, geology, meterology, archaeology, liturgics, and cooking. Most importantly, the tyro bards would spend most of their time doing another (non-verbal) job, and, in the evenings, tend an animal and a garden (Auden 1963). Evidently, Auden thought mastering the language the first priority – but then came something to write about (rather than just lyricizing the self), and time entirely free of poetic concerns, letting ideas stew.

Alas, in UK departments of creative writing, universities face the difficult job of reconciling standards voiced by professional poets with student dreams of self-expression, and those with government interest in employability and transferable skills. Though interest in and provision for creative writing has soared in the last ten years, keeping goats, earthing up spuds, and chanting matins are still only dreams. Courses face questions about whether creativity can be taught or only encouraged; if it can, whether it is worth teaching to most creative writing students, who do not go on to writing careers; whether it is a distinct area of knowledge about the world, open to intellectual analysis, or an apprenticeship; whether it should focus on responses to reading or on technical exercises in writing (Harper 2006). In fact, these queries merely run over old ground in the ancient art of rhetoric, the focus of education until the nineteenth century. Cicero and Quintilian come down firmly on the side of improving natural talents of speech by study. They provide systematic exercises to do this (varying the grammatical form of a sentence, for instance, or taking a topic through logical predicates). Moreover, they expect the neophyte orator to take his skills into other areas of study and life, as a good citizen of the republic (Vickers 1988). If they looked over our creative writing programmes, only the expectations that some students have of therapeutic writing might cause them to snort.

The English Subject Centre report on creative writing at universities argued that the aim of a degree in this discipline is to develop a combined critical and writerly understanding of fictional genres and the imaginative possibilities of language (Michelene Wandor, in Holland et al. 2003, 13). Generally, the primary teaching mode is the workshop, where samples of student work are circulated beforehand. Its authors get detailed feedback in the workshop from peers and tutors, then all participants attempt a writing exercise in class. Typically, the student is also required to reflect on the processes by which the creative piece was produced. Such an environment emphasizes trust and collaboration, where students' comments are expected to be specific and constructive (analogous to fine art studios). Indeed, the English Subject Centre recommended that skills developed in the visual and performing arts be considered when drafting writing programmes: in recognizing and developing new ideas; in dealing with cross-media, cross-discipline complexity; in dealing with the interface between emotion, experience, and intellect; in accommodating the tension between theory and practice; in professional standard presentation and well-developed entrepreneurial and business skills; and, most demandingly of all, in a general capacity to be bold, take risks, and show breadth of vision (Holland et al. 2003, 9).

The Practice of Writers

So there are plenty of ideas about what might make a creative space, in the literary and the wider worlds. However, this collection is the first to compare the *practice* of a number of writers, asking how their environment co-operates in the act of writing. It should, therefore, go some way to testing the theories.

Poe's 1846 essay on how he wrote 'The Raven' is a warning to those brave people today who ask questions about a poet's inspiration and work methods at the end of a poetry reading. Determining to write a poem to suit popular and critical taste, Poe starts with its length: not too long to be read at one sitting, he thinks, so best one hundred lines. Now for the subject: since beauty (not truth or passion) is the point of a poem, and melancholy produces a particular beauty, then melancholy it is. Refrains effect this, but need varying in application to stop boredom, so they need to be short and sonorous. 'Nevermore' fits the bill, but then he needs a pretext for using it so often – a raven, perhaps, since a parrot is not in keeping with the tone? This just leaves the lover's queries, as the context to vary the repeated refrain, and it will all be done. There is just enough serendipity in this account to make one pause before calling it mock-serious. Citing Wordsworth's definition of poetry as the 'spontaneous overflow of powerful feelings,' on subjects which the poet has also 'thought long and deeply,' and Burns's confession that poetry composed by his will rather than his wish had never succeeded, A. E. Housman prescribed a lunchtime beer ('beer is a sedative to the brain, and my afternoons are the least intellectual portion of my life') with an after-lunch meander so ideas could bubble up (Ghiselin 1952, 90, 82). Authors, past and present, have a canny and amused self-consciousness of when they can let themselves go off with the faeries and when they need, in Trollope's phrase, to stick themselves to a chair with cobbler's wax. Inspiration is partnered by the pragmatic business of writing, whatever you they feel like.

Imagine then, if you will, the English Association's first virtual literary festival, where a starry cast come to talk about their work. A group photo first, for the webpage: from left to right, seated, Mrs Margaret Oliphant, Miss Charlotte Brontë, Miss Emily Brontë, Mr John Milton, and standing, Mr Ben Jonson, Mr Anthony Trollope, Mr W. H. Auden, Mr Andrew Motion. Hovering anxiously behind them are their minders, our contributors, scanning the audience for the awkward squad as we open the question session.

Q1: Where do your best ideas come from? Generally, authors muse, they get them when they let themselves step aside from the world of action. Auden retreats into a cave of making, Charlotte Brontë puts herself into a trance, Trollope (to some rib-poking from Jonson) admits to dreaming about his characters all through the day, Oliphant relies on 'fantasticating', even when she's in a sewing circle.

Q2: So you have to be alone to write? There's agreement among the men that in bed, or at least first thing in the morning, is when they get most of their work done. Milton is milked of the verses that come to him after he has woken up, Trollope is at his desk by 5.30 am, and even Auden and Motion, somnolent moderns, manage to start by 8.00. The women seem to have other things to do first thing in the morning. Oliphant waits until her household has gone to bed before she starts writing, the Brontës think through their work together in the evenings.

Q3: Do you take anything to make you more creative? [Pause, as youthful questioner is ejected.] Jonson is quite clear that you need the sociable environment of the tavern to smash through any rigidities of thought. He gets wholehearted support from Auden, who recommends a 'few labour-saving devices [that] have been introduced into the mental kitchen – alcohol, coffee, tobacco, Benzedrine' (Auden 1963). The rest of the group cough discreetly.

Q4: Does your day job interfere with your writing? The group is mixed on this one. While many agree with Motion's contention that poetry ('and novels,' remind others) is fundamentally part of life, they also find it difficult when 'doing' life to get space to concentrate on its significance. Milton and Trollope point out proudly that they are currently working in very senior jobs in the civil service, where their efforts will affect hundreds of thousands of people. Auden interjects that at least, then, they have something to write about, and distributes prospectuses for the Bangor Bardic College.

Q5: Who are your influences? The previous question seems to linger in the minds of the authors, who point out that though poetry may not pay, writing masques, journalism, reviews, travel guides, and biography does. They enjoy the variety. All the group stress how important it is to read widely and deeply, and to discuss new ideas with peers, but Jonson, Auden, Oliphant, and Motion also do this for a living.

Q6: How do you know when a poem is finished? There is strong agreement that proper revision comes about when each author can make her writing strange to herself. Motion and Auden (and perhaps Jonson also) use print technology to defamiliarize their work. They, Oliphant, and the Brontë sisters find that reading a first draft to another person also makes for a thorough critique. Milton, of course, relies on another's voice to hear his work for the first time after dictation. Only Trollope stays silent, muttering that he doesn't like 'the smell of the polishing oil.'

Q7: *What do you do when you're feeling uncreative?* Cries of 'Have a drink,' 'Have a chat,' 'Nip off for a walk,' and then – without exception – '*Come back and get on with it.*'

Go to any literary reading now, and the answers will be the same: writers need time and space to re-perceive the world, a 'tough but nice' group of people to listen to their drafts, a revision process that makes the work strange, and, above all, persistence. 'Doing' literature takes a doughty personality as much as a sensitive soul. Put in less rococo terms, the essays in this collection focus on these specific, material aspects of the author's work-in-progress.

Stan Smith's chapter on W. H. Auden starts with a warning that poets and their readers work up a group fantasy that they can see poems growing under a poet's fingers, in the 'right now' of the poem. As Smith has said in conversation, this mythological present, abstracted from the precise physical circumstances of composition, produces an immaculate conception of the poem and a corresponding poetry of immaculate conception. By contrast, Smith describes the concrete detail of Auden's habits of collaborative and multi-media writing, from typist errors to collage to friends' critiques. The poet, retreating to write in a curtained room regardless of its state, was self-disciplined about his hours of work. Coolly incisive, controlled poetry and essays emerged from an 'Auden-scape ... of stale coffee grounds, tarry nicotine, and toe-jam.' The Victorian novelist Margaret Oliphant, whom Elisabeth Jay surveys, would be horrified at the prospective amount of clearing up in the wake of such a mess. Jay points out how difficult it was for Oliphant to get time and space away from domestic duties, physical and social, in order to write. Given the household income came entirely from her work, she kept in close touch with her publishers, who allowed her to try her hand – at breakneck speed – at lucrative reviewing and travel writing as well as fiction. A regime of night-work, often in bed, evolved to allow her to put the products of her 'fantasticating' or daydreaming down on paper. Yet her family situation was core to her creative environment. Mirroring her own movement in and out of the domestic circle, Oliphant became adept in moving between characters' inner thoughts and how they were perceived by their family and friends. She read each day's work out at night to her family, first her mother and brother, later to the generation below her, and looked forward with excitement to their criticisms. Once again, though, the main quality displayed is tenacity. Oliphant kept on writing, whether she was up an Alp or in the swim in London society.

Of all the authors dealt with here, though, Anthony Trollope most inspires in me a tonic mingling of envy and exhaustion. He balanced his writing with the highly efficient conduct of the most senior posts in the British Post Office (it was he, for instance, who introduced the postbox here). N. John Hall's chapter shows how a habit of rapid, one-draft composition was developed by the report-writing Trollope did in his character of postal district Surveyor, and how orderly office habits proved highly productive: Trollope would wake early to write his target word count (some ten pages daily), duly regulated by being recorded in working diaries, with a watch on the table before him, before going into the Post Office. As with Oliphant, the range of topics and genres he covered seemed to invigorate him, not just novels, but also travel books, biographies, articles, and reviews. Yet, against this extraordinary appetite for action came another side to his creativity: daydreaming while walking for pleasure, riding on official duties, reading or eating. He was continually asking himself how this or that character would behave given the story so far.

The home at Haworth takes a very different complexion to the ordered, outward-looking spaces which supported Trollope and Oliphant, in Stevie Davies's chapter on Charlotte and Emily Brontë. Childhood games changed in adulthood into a visionary world that met the wild world around the parsonage, both giving matter to write. At Haworth, as with other writers, the family was an initial audience, supportive and critical. Primarily, however, the sisters made for each other a force-field of creativity, all balancing individual privacy with corporate thought, circling the dining room table each evening as they planned the progress of their work.

John Milton's dependence on women was less positive. Peter C. Herman's chapter contrasts the difficulties felt on both sides by the blind man and his daughters. Milton used his daughters to read out sources he wanted to consult, and to take dictation of his emerging drafts. Much of what they read out was in a language the women did not understand, another factor in an already strained relationship. By contrast, Milton's Muse is described as a woman whose help he warmly welcomes. Herman examines how depending on such voices outside him gave resonance to Milton's epic as a play of voices, which can change emphasis or even contradict each other over such major issues as how the Son of God gained pre-eminence or why man first fell into sin. Yet, Herman notes, despite the political failures, family unhappiness, and financial worries which make up the background of the poem's genesis, the literary heritage industry, from the nineteenth century to today, proffers images of a serene Milton rising above his circumstances, surrounded by loving women.

With Adam Smyth and Michelle O'Callaghan's essay on Ben Jonson the interest shifts to public scenes of writing. One might expect that the 1600s habit of talking over ideas with cronies in a tavern would encourage collaborative writing, and indeed it does, in plays and witty extempore verse. More surprising to modern ears, though, is the way that libraries are also public places of composition, where readers come to meet other scholars, not to get away from them into a private and silent space. The codes of behaviour governing the psycho-geography of tavern and library are explored against the confined space of Jonson's desk, ink and sealing wax to hand.

What of those whose business is the business of writing? The penumbra of the creative environment is explored in the interviews Graeme Harper did with people in a literary archive, a literary festival, a literary web magazine, two literary heritage sites, and a literary public role. Andrew Motion reflects on his writers' block, partly brought on by trying to change the post of Poet Laureate from a figurehead who writes occasional poetry to a leader and catalyst for literature. Motion is committed to the idea that poetry is absolutely part of life, not away from it, but moves at different speeds to life; it concentrates the mind. He works best when his physical situation mirrors this: first thing in the morning, in a small flat, leaving the poems to stew quietly alone for a while. The externalized energy and theatricality required for the Laureateship engage him with life, but also distance him from the silent concentration needed to reflect on it.

However, it is this very pizzazz which inspires Peter Florence, the Director of the Hay Literary Festival. The original event in Hay-on-Wye has continued, drawing upwards of 80,000 people each year, but the festival also now runs at the Alhambra in Granada, Spain and in Cartagena in Columbia. The locations (rural Welsh national park, medieval Islamic palace complex, and Spanish colonial walled fort) might suggest an uneasy mixture of literary workshop with beauty-spot tourism (a busman's holiday, it might seem to most teachers and dons). However, Florence emphasizes that the wonder inspired by the surroundings and the fun of a holiday – even the playpen stuff of camping in the mud – are the two primary creative elements of the festival. They allow a re-perception of the meanings of the environ-ment, and dissolve boundaries in thinking about literature and its place in the world. There is a direct link between the open-mindedness that 'gets' literature and a receptiveness to good wine, smart comedians, and political adventure.

Conservation and recycling of the passing moment of composition concerns both Jamie Andrews, Head of Modern Literary Manuscripts at the British Library, and Robert Sheppard, who is a poet and critic, and edits a blog-zine. Both are concerned with how to select material to conserve, to exhibit, or to mount on the web, what to do about e-traces of authorship in digital texts, and what effect making these available to the public has on further composition. The difference between heritage value and literary value becomes clearer in the choices posed by limits of time (for the blogger) and money (for the archivist). Do you preserve a picture of the daily life of a reader (in the case of the blogger) or a picture of the daily life of British literary heritage (in the case of the archivist), regardless of quality? Or do you only preserve the greats? Quality control, says Sheppard gloomily, is key: cyberspace junk litters the blogosphere. Finally, both consider what happens to new work when a reader sees in concrete detail the hesitations and deviations that go into a familiar piece.

Then comes an area where education and entertainment sidle towards each other: those literary heritage sites which are reused for modern productions. Farah Karim-Cooper, of Shakespeare's Globe in London, and Kate Rumbold, of the Shakespeare Institute in Stratford, discuss the multiple Shakespeares which result when the economic and aesthetic – the heritage and the theatrical – aspects to the value we give Shakespeare are split off. Their conclusions are echoed in Graeme Harper's Postscript, which warns against too rigorous an ethnography of creativity.

Results Guaranteed?

Though this collection stresses the material nature of the creative environment it is *not* a recipe book which considers inspiration irrelevant. The trajectory of trust in this element has been sustained from classical entreaties to the Muse to breathe poetry through one's lips (or, alternatively, guarding against her trollopy kisses), to Renaissance visions of the golden world above the dirty quotidian of history, to Romantic hopes for a spontaneous overflow of emotion on recognizing the innate divinity of the natural world. Such idealism has always gone hand in hand with careful training in verbal forms; literature involves both transcendence (*ekstasis*) and art (*techne*).

This type of criticism appears more rarely now. The material age produced a secular literary theory, characterized in most concrete terms by Ezra Pound's 'A Few Don'ts' for those beginning to write verse (use no superfluous word, no adjective, which does not reveal something ... go in fear of abstractions ... don't imagine that a thing will 'go' in verse just because it's too dull to go in prose ...). This does not come from a manly reserve about telling others how the Muse comes to them, on the part of poets, novelists, and dramatists. It comes from recognizing that all features of the external world can inspire, both the ideal and material.

Works Cited

Amabile, Teresa, 1996. *Creativity in Context*. Boulder, CO: Westview Press.
Auden, W. H., 1963. *The Dyer's Hand and Other Essays*. London: Faber & Faber.
Bilton, Chris, 2007. *Management and Creativity: From Creative Industries to Creative Management*. Oxford: Blackwell.
Caves, Richard, 2000. *Creative Industries: Contracts Between Art and Commerce*. Cambridge, MA: Harvard University Press.
Florida, Richard, 2002. *The Rise of the Creative Class and How It's Transforming Work, Leisure, Community, and Everyday Life*. New York: Basic Books.
Freud, Sigmund, 1959. 'Creative Writers and Daydreaming' (1908), trans. and ed. J. Strachey, *The Standard Edition of the Complete Psychological Works of Sigmund Freud*, vol. 9. London: Hogarth Press.
Ghiselin, Brewster, 1952. *The Creative Process: A Symposium*. Berkeley: University of California Press.
GLAM. http://archives.li.man.ac.uk/glam/index.html
Harper, Graeme, ed., 2006. *Teaching Creative Writing*. London: Continuum.
Hartley, John, 2005. *The Creative Industries*. Oxford: Blackwell.
Heartfield, James, 2000. *Great Expectations: The Creative Industries in the New Economy*. London: Design Agenda.
Henry, Jane, ed., 2006. *Creative Management and Development*. London: Open University/Sage.
Holland, Siobhan, et al., 2003. *Creative Writing: A Good Practice Guide*. London: English Subject Centre.
Landry, Charles, 2000. *The Creative City: A Toolkit for Urban Innovators*. London: Earthscan.
Larkin, Philip, 1979. 'A Neglected Responsibility: Contemporary Literary Manuscripts,' *Encounter*, 53.1 (1979): 33–40.
Maslow, Abraham, 1976. 'Creativity in Self-actualising People,' in Albert Rothenberg and Carl Hausman, eds, *The Creativity Question*. Durham, NC: Duke University Press.

Poe, Edgar Allan, 2007. 'The Philosophy of Composition' (1846), in S. and S. F. Levine, eds, *Edgar Allan Poe: Critical Theory, the Major Documents*. Urbana: University of Illinois Press.

Vickers, Brian, 1988. *In Defence of Rhetoric*. Oxford: Clarendon Press.

Wallas, Graham, 1926. *The Art of Thought*. London: Jonathan Cape.

Winnicott, D. W., 1971. *Playing and Reality*. London: Tavistock Publications.

Gubbins at a Desk: Auden's Cave

STAN SMITH

What the World Likes

There you go, writers all the time – the kind of people who are forever at home. Gubbins at a desk. It would do you good to understand that very few people give tuppence for your Mr Eliot, plus all the writers in Christendom. Dancing. Parties. Sport. That is what the world likes.

THUS THE MOTHER of Christopher Logue in his autobiographical memoir (Logue 1999, 4). Poets are indeed largely homebodies and, though some have composed standing in front of a typewriter, and Wordsworth elaborated his convoluted sentences out loud while walking, the writing of poems is largely a sedentary occupation. 'Plainly, / ours is a sitting culture,' wrote W. H. Auden, and 'would rather incline its buttocks / on a well-upholstered chair' (Auden 1966, 46–7). Where writers sit when they write is, then, an important consideration, frequently entering into the very mise-en-scène of a poem.

Take Coleridge's conversation poems, for instance, which appear to insist on the immediacy of poetic presence, the writer caught for ever in the very act of writing, as in the opening of 'Frost at Midnight' in a calm which nevertheless 'disturbs / And vexes meditation.' That tension between calm and vexation arises in fact straight out of the poem's double life, its textual bilocation, claiming to speak directly from the poet's midnight moment, while actually turning its tricks in the always original present of each new reader. Vexation seems to have been central to Coleridge's poetic genius. 'This Lime Tree Bower my Prison,' which again opens in the allegedly immediate present of its composition ('Well, they are gone, and here must I remain'), originated from a domestic accident which now, to the modern reader, seems like a subversively comic footnote to the ideology of Romantic inspiration: his wife Sarah had spilt a skillet of boiling milk on his foot. Similarly, as his prefatory note to 'Kubla Khan' records, it was the arrival of 'a person on business from Porlock' that cut short that poem's completion. Another vexation, however, was responsible for the poem's very genesis, for which opium was only the contingent occasion. The 'anodyne had been prescribed,' Coleridge says, 'In consequence of a slight indisposition,' 'from the effects' of which 'he fell asleep in his chair.' A second, manuscript note is more specific, revealing that the poem was 'composed, in a sort of Reverie brought on by two grains of Opium taken to check a dysentery' (Coleridge 1963, 164). Perhaps the poet was cut short in more than one sense, then, and we shouldn't enquire too closely where exactly he was sitting while he wrote. As Auden remarks, 'From the manuscript evidence, it now appears that Coleridge's account of the composition of "Kubla Khan" was a fib' ('Writing,' Auden 1975, 16).

Auden's own poem 'The Geography of the House' opens playfully with him apparently 'Seated after breakfast / In this white-tiled cabin / Arabs call *the House where / Everybody goes*' (Auden 1966, 26). But it proceeds to slam the door on our intrusion, turning the sentence into a generalization about how 'Even melancholics / Raise a cheer to Mrs. / Nature' in the loo. In his 'Letter to Lord Byron,' the epistolary mode adds credibility to the claim that he is sitting on an Icelandic quayside and 'writing this in pencil on my knee' (Auden and MacNeice 1937, 49). But in the very process of making the claim, the real history of the poem's production is dissimulated. 'What the world likes' from a poem is a sense of being actually – impossibly – there, as the poet sees, feels and writes. In such encounters we relish that most elusive of ideological chimeras, the illusion of presence. But Auden's reflections in 'Making, Knowing and Judging' are more to the point here: 'Even if poems were often written in trances, poets would still accept responsibility for them by signing their names and taking the credit. They cannot claim oracular immunity. Admirers of "Kubla Khan" … should not lightly dismiss what Coleridge … says in his introductory note,' that it was merely 'a psychological curiosity' published only because Lord Byron had urged him to. Coleridge saw that 'even the fragment that exists is disjointed and would have had to be worked on if he ever completed the poem, and his critical conscience felt on its honor to admit this' (Auden 1975, 33). However and wherever writers are sitting when they first put pen to paper, this is an arbitrary extrapolation from a creative process which precedes and succeeds the moment of writing.

Christopher Logue recalls hearing Samuel Beckett describe, with some fascination, Balzac's writing practices:

'He worked on the first floor. On either side of his table there was a hole in the floor. On the floor below, his printers. When he finished a page he dropped it through the hole on his right and began the next. Later, his pages came up through the hole on his left as proofs to be corrected, dropped back down, then printed and published.'

(Logue 1999, 174)

However, the narrator's double-take at the end of Beckett's novel *Molloy* admits to the real story of literary composition: 'I went back into the house and wrote. It is midnight. The rain is beating on the windows. It was not midnight. It was not raining.' 'I speak in the present tense,' Molloy had observed earlier, 'it is so easy to speak in the present tense, when speaking of the past. It is the mythological present, don't mind it' (Beckett 1979, 162, 26). All texts, no matter where their speakers allege they are sitting as they speak, exist in the mythological present, and cannot be trusted to tell the truth about either their own inception or the present they claim to present to us.

In the Dark Room

Poems are born liars, endlessly dissembling their locations, ringing home to say they'll be working late at the office when they're already drinking in the bar. Consider that most widely quoted of last century's suppressed poems, one which underwent an astonishing resurrection after 9/11: Auden's 'September 1, 1939.' It opens:

> I sit in one of the dives
> On Fifty-second Street
> Uncertain and afraid
> As the clever hopes expire
> Of a low dishonest decade.   (Auden 1940, 112)

Unlike those 'faces along the bar' who 'cling to their average day,' the poet appears to be fairly sober. He knows what lies ahead for all of them, even in New York's 'neutral air.' And he knows exactly where he is. And so, we believe, do we. He is sitting in a bar on Fifty-Second Street, writing a poem about the uncertain future of a world plunged into war by Hitler's invasion of Poland. The poem maintains a sedate sense of the importance and solemnity of the occasion. This is the real thing, in which the simultaneity of sitting and writing testify to the urgency of the moment.

We even have eye-witness testimony to the poet's presence in the memoirs of Harold Norse, the young man who was then still the regular boyfriend of Auden's new and thereafter lifelong muse and lover, Chester Kallman:

> At the end of August … Chester and I spent our first night at a notorious gay bar called the Dizzy Club on West Fifty-second Street. … The dive was the sex addict's quick fix, packed to the rafters with college boys and working-class youth under twenty-five. From street level you stepped into a writhing mass of tight boys in tighter pants. On those sultry August nights it was a sexual experience just getting a drink. Like the subway at rush hour you were crushed against one another. … Amid the laughter and screaming and ear-splitting jukebox music, it was like an orgy room for the fully clad. Everything but exposure and nudity took place. (Norse 1990, 78)

This is not quite as the poet describes it, but some poetic licence is perhaps allowable. We can be sure, though, that the poet sat in that dive and wrote that poem, just as the poem asserts with its insistent present tense. After all, we have Norse's word for it:

> Having decided that he must see it, we told Wystan, who loved sleazy dives, about the Dizzy Club. The next night, September 1, without our knowledge he went alone. I can only imagine what occurred there. With floppy shoelaces, creased suit and tie, ash-stained, he must have looked out of place, though with his rosy California tan and sun-bleached hair he could, in the right light, pass for twenty-five. He didn't go to pick up a boy; however, aware of the age difference and quite shy, he would have selected one of the two unused corner tables at the rear of the bar, which was usually deserted except for those too drunk to stand, from which he could observe boys kissing and groping under the bright lights, packed like sardines pickled in alcohol. There he would begin to write the most famous poem of the decade. Surely he jotted notes, or even the first stanzas, for it begins with the immediacy of composition in situ. He did not write a detailed description of his immediate surroundings or his personal feelings, but instead opened the poem outward into society at that historic moment, choosing the depressed mood of his isolation within the social drama. At precisely this moment, while Auden wrote tracing fascism and its 'psychopathic gods' from Martin Luther to the birth of Hitler at Linz, the German Führer marched into Poland and started World War II. The poem was, of course, 'September 1, 1939.' (Norse 1990, 79)

On second thoughts, it appears that all we have *is* Norse's word for it, for all the circumstantiating thick detail. This is a speculative riff, not eye-witness, reconstructed retrospectively on the basis of what he's read in the poem and what he knows about the Dizzy Club, embroidered by a taste for camp hyperbole, and steeped in a subjunctive mode which leaves the poem's genesis shrouded in beer-stained mystery. What a reader wants is precisely what Norse waves under his nose and then withdraws: a prospect onto 'the immediacy of composition in situ.'

As editor of the little magazine *New Verse*, which did so much to establish Auden's reputation in the forefront of 1930s writing, Geoffrey Grigson recognized that it is as a 'new verbal actuality' that a text finds its real placement. Some Gubbins has to sit down at a desk and inscribe inky marks on a blank sheet. Other Gubbinses have to work to set it up for publication. The materiality of poetic production is no mystery to an editor – or to anyone who has struggled with Auden's small, neat, but often inscrutable handwriting:

> Within a few years … poems were coming to me from Birmingham or from the Malverns, and I was publishing them in *New Verse*. They came on half sheets of notepaper, on long sheets of lined foolscap, in writing that an airborne daddy-longlegs might have managed with one dangling leg, sometimes in pencil, sometimes smudged and still less easy to decipher. They had to be typed before they went to the printer, and in the act of typing each poem established itself. It was rather like old-fashioned developing in the dark-room, but more certain, more exacting. ('A Meaning of Auden', Spender 1975, 14)

The translation from script to print, through all its various stages, is the 'true' birthing of a poem, until 'there at last on the white page, to be clearer still on the galley, the first entire sight of a new poem joining our literature' (Spender 1975, 14). But there are quite a few helping hands in that dark room.

Mutual Services

Stephen Spender's limited edition of Auden's *Poems* (1928) was laboriously set by Spender himself on 'a small hand press of a kind, I later learned, used sometimes for printing chemists' labels.' It was, he recalled, 'abominably printed … a lot of the typography has letters only half of which are printed … [and] several copies contain corrections … sometimes of words, in Auden's or my handwriting' (Sutherland 2005, 84). Auden himself, in his reflections on 'Writing,' gave a characteristically pungent account of how the transfer from script to print could affect the destiny of a poem:

> Most people enjoy the sight of their own handwriting as they enjoy the smell of their own farts. Much as I loathe the typewriter, I must admit that it is a help in self-criticism. Typescript is so impersonal and hideous to look at that, if I type out a poem, I immediately see defects which I missed when I looked through it in manuscript.
>
> (Auden 1975, 17)[1]

Norse records a transitional moment in January 1940 when, typing up Auden's handwritten draft of 'New Year Letter,' he inadvertently omitted a line. The circumstances of that mistake (including sexual rivalry) are vividly evoked:

> One day, as I sat at work in the living room while Wystan and Chester caroused in the bedroom with a bottle of wine amid loud laughter and campy conversation, my fingers struck the keys like a pianist in the mad climax of an onrushing crescendo. I was eager to finish and join them. Finally I completed the ten or so pages of octo-syllabic couplets and called through the half-open bedroom door, 'Wystan, I'm finished.' He emerged, took the pencilled manuscript and typescript, remarking on its neatness and absence of erasures … handed me some correspondence to type, and returned to the bedroom. Again I heard the easy laughter and conversation. Then, abruptly, the laughter ceased, followed by a long silence. I assumed they were making love while I plodded on, when suddenly Wystan burst into the living room in a towering rage.
> 'You've ruined the manuscript!' he screamed. 'You left out a line! Why the hell didn't you go over it, for God's sake? His voice, growing more hysterical, rose in volume and pitch. 'The whole damn poem is in rhymed couplets so you could have easily detected a missing line! It's ruined!'
> This was too much. … 'It was the only mistake,' I muttered with choked resentment. 'I can retype it, but I'm leaving!' … my eyes blurring with tears. Torn between shame and fury Wystan glared nervously, puffing compulsively at his cigarette. He fumbled in his trousers for the wages, paid me, and I fled. (Norse 1990, 88)

---

[1]   By the time he shared a house with Charles Miller in Ann Arbor in 1940–41, teaching at the University of Michigan, Auden was reconciled to the typewriter: 'he sat every morning in the living room behind a closed door, tapping out the first pages of For the [Time] Being on his European portable' (Miller 1989, 15).

'Lucky the poet whose collected works are not full of misprints,' Auden wrote in 'Making, Knowing and Judging,' adding that 'the invention of printing' has not 'made editors unnecessary.' 'Even a young poet knows soon or very soon will realize that, but for scholars, he would be at the mercy of the literary taste of a past generation, since, once a book has gone out of print and been forgotten, only the scholar with his unselfish courage to read the unreadable will retrieve the rare prize' (Auden 1975, 43). Editors and scholars are thus demiurgic step-parents of a poet's texts, reinventing them for new generations. Auden's first editions are notoriously prone to misprints, some of them only finally corrected when Edward Mendelson produced his edition of the *Collected Poems* in 1976. Initial printings of the *Selected Poems* (1979, 1981) duplicate the same line between stanzas 3 and 4 of 'River Profile,' an error occasioned because the third line of every stanza ends with the word 'country.' The poem makes absolute sense with the repeated line, and a case could be made for it on stylistic grounds. This kind of error, according to Sebastiano Timpanaro, is so well known to textual scholars that it has its own name, *saut de l'un à l'autre*, in which the compositor's eye, hexed by the recurrence of a word or phrase, picks up the wrong place to start again. Sometimes, however, with Auden, a compositor's intervention could be retained in a poem's final version. A printer's error substituted the word 'ports' for the original 'poets' in the opening poem of *Letters from Iceland*. Auden preferred the seren-dipitous over-correction, and the line now reads 'And the ports have names for the sea.'

Auden engaged in collaborative writing throughout his career, from early experiments like the 'Oxford Collective Poem' Charles Madge described in *New Verse* (Madge 1937, 16–19; Smith 2009), through joint authorship with MacNeice in *Letters from Iceland* and with Isher-wood in the 1930s plays and *Journey to a War*, to the collaboration on the libretti with Kallman. The thirties drama required close creative co-operation with producers and directors like Rupert Doone, whose avant-garde Group Theatre performed (and adapted) the plays. Docu-mentaries like *Night Mail* for the GPO Film Unit likewise involved collective work. Christopher Isherwood recorded, presciently, in the *New Verse* double number dedicated to Auden in 1937, that he was

> still much preoccupied with ritual, in all its forms. When we collabo-rate, I have to keep a sharp eye on him – or down flop the characters on their knees (see 'F.6' passim): another constant danger is that of

choral interruptions by angel-voices. If Auden had his way, he would
turn every play into a cross between grand opera and high mass.

(Isherwood 1937, 4)

It was generally thought that, in his collaborations with Isherwood,
there was a clear demarcation between the latter's prose and Auden's
verse. Recent work on the diaries that formed the basis of the prose in
Journey to a War has revealed that Auden had a bigger hand in these
than was previously realized. Similar findings have been mooted of the
prose passages in the drama.

Work with Kallman on the libretti also required genuine multi-media
interaction with composers, choreographers, and singers, often, as with
Bunyan and *Billy Budd*, pre-existing friends like Benjamin Britten and
Peter Pears, or those like Igor Stravinsky befriended during the process
of collaboration. Thekla Clark reports that

> Collaboration soon developed its own routine. Ordinarily in Kirch-
> stetten Wystan worked in his 'cave' and Chester outside, but they
> used the cocktail table when they worked together. Neither was a
> bustler nor a brooder, but when collaborating they were like two
> concerned hens. They delighted in the work. I remember shrieks
> of laughter and Chester saying, 'You couldn't' and Wystan 'What a
> pity.' (Clark 1995, 89–90)

Louis Kronenberger recalls, of their collaboration on the *Faber Book
of Aphorisms*, that the only feasible place for sorting out their accumulated file cards was 'the floor of my study. The ensuing three hours, if
photographed or filmed, might have revealed two late-middle-aged and
obviously crack-brained men sprawled out on the floor and engaged in a
very punitive or pathological game of slapjack … in the midst of which
my wife entered to announce that Edmund Wilson had just phoned
asking whether he could come up for a drink,' to be told '"Wystan and
Louis are sprawled out on the floor sorting their aphorisms"' ('A friendship revisited,' Spender 1975, 156–7).

Besides such 'formal' collaborations, Auden had a more informal
method of plugging friends into the act of composition. A rather more
radical practice than simply seeking their opinion and alternative
suggestions for words or images, it issued in collages made up of phrases
they approved of, as Isherwood confided in *New Verse*:

> When Auden was younger he was very lazy. He hated polishing and
> making corrections. If I didn't like a poem, he threw it away and

wrote another. If I liked one line, he would keep it and work it into a new poem. In this way, whole poems were constructed which were simply anthologies of my favourite lines, entirely regardless of grammar or sense. This is the simple explanation of much of Auden's celebrated obscurity. (Isherwood 1937, 6)

In constructing the neophyte's own inner critical 'Censor,' according to 'Making, Knowing and Judging,' some things can be learnt only from his contemporaries, 'with whom he shares one thing in common, youth':

The apprentices do each other a ... mutual service which no older and sounder critic could do. They read each other's manuscripts. At this age a fellow apprentice has two great virtues as a critic. When he reads your poem, he may grossly overestimate it, but if he does, he really believes what he is saying; he never flatters or praises merely to encourage. Secondly, he reads your poem with that passionate atten-tion which grown-up critics only give to masterpieces and grown-up poets only to themselves. When he finds fault, his criticisms are intended to help you to improve. He really wants your poem to be better. It is just this kind of personal criticism which in later life, when the band of apprentices has dispersed, a writer often finds it so hard to get ... A critic's duty is to tell the public what a work is, not tell its author what he should and could have written instead. Yet this is the only kind of criticism from which an author can benefit.
(Auden 1975, 40–1)

The essay even indulges in a Balzacian fantasy of corporate *atelier* production:

If poetry were in great demand so that there were overworked profes-sional poets, I can imagine a system under which an established poet would take on a small number of apprentices who would begin by changing his blotting paper, advance to typing his manuscripts and end up by ghostwriting poems for him which he was too busy to start or finish. (Auden 1975, 37)

Changes of political and cultural fashion obviously form part of the material conditions of textual manufacture, as with Auden's revisions and final suppression of poems such as 'Spain' and 'September 1, 1939' in the aftermath of the Nazi–Soviet Pact. Sometimes, however, quite trivial practicalities can affect not only a book's production but also, thereafter, the precise terms of its consumption. A book's title is a key part of its meaning, conditioning a reader's perception of its themes and structure. Auden's 1936 collection *Look, Stranger!* confirmed his national reputation and earned him the King's Gold Medal for Poetry in 1937. Nicholas Jenkins has traced in the Faber archives how the book's English title, which Auden always disowned, was fabricated and imposed on him by Eliot and his fellow editors (Jenkins 2005, 18–23). Auden subsequently instructed his American publisher to amend the title to *On this Island* for the US edition, adding: 'Faber invented a bloody title while I was away without telling me. It sounds like the work of a vegetarian lady novelist' (Carpenter 1981, 204). Faber didn't like any of Auden's proposed titles, and he in turn rejected all their suggestions, facetiously proposing in some exasperation that 'On the analogy of [Eliot's] *Burnt Norton*, I might call it *Piddle-in-the-hole*.' At this point, to Faber's evident relief, Auden's departure to Iceland, to write the travelogue Faber had commissioned, opened a window of opportunity. Eliot wrote to Auden in Birmingham on 18 June 1936, no doubt aware that he had already departed for Iceland, requesting alternative titles and proposing some of Faber's own. Auden's mother, who was acting as unpaid secretary, replied the next day that she was forwarding the letter to Iceland. 'Meanwhile,' Jenkins writes, 'the manufacturing process began.' On 3 July, Miss Cowling, a secretary to Richard de la Mare, Faber's production director, wrote to Mrs Auden asking her to correct the page proofs of 'your son's POEMS,' enclosing two copies of the proofs and the original manuscript, and adding that the proofs would also be corrected by 'one of our readers.' She added that 'The title of the book is wrong at present, as we are waiting to hear from him what he would like it changed to.' Mrs Auden replied immediately that she was unable to cope with these issues and had therefore sent one copy of the proofs to Wystan in Iceland. He replied to Eliot promptly, suggesting two new possible titles.

By mid-August, however, in Auden's continuing absence, the editors had already decided on a title of their own. On his return in September, Auden protested about this cavalier treatment, to be informed by Frank Morley, to whom his complaint had been passed, that it was now 'too late to make any change. We were in great difficulty about the title, because you had just gone to Iceland and we couldn't consult you about it. … [A]s we are too late to change, there isn't much that I can say, except that I hope it won't do any harm.' 'Scholarship cannot afford to forget the actually existing conditions under which books were and are written and made,' Jenkins comments, 'But Morley was wrong to say that Faber did not receive Auden's title in time to have used it: they must either have overlooked, forgotten or rejected [it].' The Faber archive reveals that the claims about not being able to consult the poet were disingenuous. In the production of this, perhaps the most famous and influential volume of poetry of the 1930s, Constance Rosalie Auden, Miss Cowling, T. S. Eliot and sundry Faber executives all had a severely practical hand, in ways that shaped its reception and interpretation ever after.

The Cave of Making

A. L. Rowse recalls a meeting with the undergraduate poet:

> After a poetry reading in the hot glare of summer sun in the inner quad at All Souls, Wystan suggested that we should adjourn to his rooms ... and continue. Arrived there, he proceeded to 'sport the oak' (shut the outer door), pull down the blinds and close the shutters, turn on the green-shaded light on his desk – and read to me, not poems, but letters from a friend of his in Mexico ... about his goings-on with the boys. (Rowse 1987, 8)

All the anecdotalists concur in recording this womb-like half-light and seclusion as Auden's preferred ambience for both writing and discussing poetry. Martin Green, noting the undergraduate's 'self-stylisation' and 'eccentricities of dandyism,' reports that Auden 'worked always by artificial light, wore eccentric hats, carried a loaded starting pistol with him, and went always for the same walk along the canal behind the gasworks' (Green 1992, 334). Nancy Spender remembers that in 1935 when Auden was a lodger with her and her then husband, the artist William Coldstream, with whom he was working at the GPO Film Unit, he would breakfast in his dressing-gown and then 'draw the blinds, turn on the electric light, eat toffees and write poetry' (Bell 1993, 1). Stephen Spender recalls his 'first appointment' in Oxford with an Auden 'seated in a darkened room with the curtains drawn, and a lamp on a table at his elbow, so that he could see me clearly and I could only see the light reflected on his pale face' (Spender 1951, 50). Spender's subsequent recollections of Auden's Greenwich Village apartment, where he lived with 'the same bareness and simplicity' as in his Oxford days, reveal that the habit persisted:

> [T]here was the same air of concentration amid untidiness, as though he scattered books, papers, ink, cigarette stubs, drinks and cups of coffee around, like pieces in a kaleidoscope which would instantly

reassemble in a symmetrical pattern within his own mind …
[O]n his mantelpiece a crucifix denoted the change in his beliefs.
As at Oxford, his curtains were still drawn to shut out the daylight,
a condition which I found hard to bear. (Spender 1951, 297–300)

One morning Spender sought to draw them aside, only to bring them
down with a clatter, to Auden's evident exasperation. MacNeice had
similar memories of Auden's 'self-imposed blackout' at Christ Church,
'then as always … busy getting on with the job. Sitting in a room all day
with the blinds drawn, reading very fast and very widely – psychology,
ethnology, *Arabia Deserta*' (MacNeice 1982, 232, 114). In 'Letter to
Lord Byron,' written on their shared trip to Iceland, Auden was efficiently brusque in describing his ideal work environment:

> For concentration I have always found
> A small room best, the curtains drawn, the light on;
> Then I can work from nine till tea-time, right on.
>   (Auden 1937, 205)

In his 1966 elegy for MacNeice in the sequence 'Thanksgiving for
a Habitat' written in the only house he ever owned, in Kirchstetten,
Lower Austria, Auden gave his fullest, most symbolically charged
account of what he calls 'our lonely dens,' those places of solitary
activity where, in a significantly passive voice, 'silence / is turned into
objects.' What the poem's title calls 'The Cave of Making' is for Auden
a self-enclosed environment, sealed off from the outside world, both
womblike and tomblike:

> For this and for all enclosures like it the archetype
>   is Weland's Stithy, an antre
> more private than a bedroom even …
> … [F]rom the Olivetti portable,
>   the dictionaries (the very
> best money can buy), the heaps of paper, it is evident
>   what must go on. Devoid of
> flowers and family photographs, all is subordinate
>   here to a function, designed to
> discourage daydreams – hence windows averted from plausible
>   videnda but admitting a light one
> could mend a watch by – and to sharpen hearing: reached by an
>   outside staircase, domestic
> noises and odours, the vast background of natural
>   life are shut off.   (Auden 1966, 18)

'Averted' and 'shut off' are the key words. The neolithic long-barrow in Oxfordshire, more commonly called Wayland's Smithy, compounds histories, linking Stone Age burials with the Saxon myth of Weland the Smith and the Middle-English idea of poet as 'maker,' for Auden saw his study as, essentially, an artisan's workshop, a forge. Clark writes that 'Wystan's "cave"' was 'isolated from the rest of the house and reached by an unpainted outside wooden staircase. ... Seeing him go either up or down those rickety stairs was a lesson in humility' (Clark 1995, 43).

Wrecking a Room

Working from nine till tea-time, right on: well, not quite. Rowse writes of the early Auden 'regularly adhering to his work-ethic – 6.30 or 7 a.m. till well into the afternoon' (Rowse 1987, 124), but else-where contrasts what he calls this 'good middle-class discipline about work' with 'the untidiness, the scruffiness, the positive grubbiness, the aura and aroma of nicotined unwashedness!' (Rowse 1987, 43). Jane Hanly, Auden's niece, recalls that on Ischia, in the 1950s, 'Wystan worked each morning after a – to me – rather indigestible breakfast of green figs and black coffee. I would sometimes hear him reading aloud (presumably from his own work),' but 'The two of us would go swim-ming in the afternoon' (Hanly 1995, 5). Clark reports that while on Ischia they 'met most mornings in town before or after the shopping ... our routines fitted nicely as the muse and a young child are equally demanding and at more or less the same hours,' adding that 'Wystan and Chester were always at Maria's for coffee around eleven, having already put in four or five hours' work. We met there to receive the day's mail which came on the morning boat' (Clark 1995, 16–17). 'When visiting, Wystan always kept to a strict routine': 'Mornings, after coffee, cigarettes and the crossword, he worked in [her husband] John's study. He closed the door and all the shutters and worked by the light of a single table lamp whose 100 watt bulb pleased him. He was silent, but somehow his presence was felt throughout the house.' 'After working all morning, Wystan came down for Campari ... promptly at 12.30, followed by lunch at one' (Clark 1995, 75).

What Rowse called Auden's 'squalid habits' had consequences for his writing as well as his domestic environment:

cigarette ash scattered down his front, all around wherever he was ... untidiness everywhere, he reduced any room he was in to a shambles, picking up coats and even carpets to pile on top of his bed; then the drink, of every kind, the necessity for it, apart from a little drug in the morning and another at night. ... He wasn't house-trained.

(Rowse 1987, 16–17)

As Rowse recognized, Auden's later-life addictions were in some part work-related: 'Wystan himself habitually took Benzedrine in the morning, to pep him up for work; and a sleeping pill at night [according to Isherwood's diaries, seconal] to send him off at once. More and more pickled in drink, he took to having a bottle of vodka at his bedside by night' (Rowse 1987, 119). The mess, too, was partly a work prac-tice. Peter Dickinson recalls the apartment in St Mark's Place as 'a gorgeous mess,' with galley proofs 'draped thickly over tables and chairs' (Dickinson 2001, 25). Charles H. Miller reports the comments of Brad Stevens, the son of friends from Ann Arbor, to whom Auden gave part-time work building bookshelves in his apartment at 7 Cornelia Street, New York:

What a mess, that apartment! He needed a large table, so he'd balanced a four-by-eight-foot plyboard on top of the small table and put rows of manuscripts, papers, mimeograph sheets, clippings, and books face down all over the plyboard surface. It seemed completely disorganized to me, but you know Wystan – he was making a book out of that mess. (Miller 1989, 97)

James Stern has some exasperated things to add on this matter.

The speed at which he could wreck a room was barely credible, certainly dangerous. ... [A] day after he had moved into our flat in New York, I had to return to pick up a manuscript. It's a fact that if it hadn't been for the pictures on the walls I wouldn't have known where I was. Frustrated burglars could not have created greater chaos: they would hardly have covered the floor with books and clothes, all the furniture with papers, and filled every receptacle, including a flower vase, with the remains of cigarettes. God, Wystan, what a mess! ('The Indispensable Presence,' Spender 1975, 124)

Charles Miller gives an evocative account (Miller 1989, 98–103) of his first visit to Auden's '"homier nest"' at 77 St Mark's Place (his last abode before moving to Austria), from its 'old russet bricks,' green marbled fireplaces and 'soot-dusted vista of rusty fire escape ladders,' to the 'unclean stove' and 'big familiar supermarket brown bag crammed and bursting with garbage, topped with pungent coffee grounds, a half-pint cream carton oozing its last come-on to cholesterol, crowding a pert tail-end of Polish sausage,' and its 'Gregorian-motored' thirties refrigerator, while 'one of Wystan's holey socks waited patiently for a mate on the [sofa's] cat-hairy cushion,' and one of his 'three known neckties curled beside a sheaf of stapled manuscript.' 'This Auden-scape reeked of stale coffee grounds, tarry nicotine, and toe-jam mixed with metro pollution and catshit, Wystanified tenement tang,' Miller reports, as Auden, his face 'as lighted and happy as I'd ever seen it,' enthused about how Trotsky had once lived in the house, having his pamphlets printed on a small press in the basement:

> From where I sat I could see Wystan's small table with his pale blue Olympia portable ringed with piles of paper, clipped sheaves of manuscript, and his cardboard student notebooks with black and white marbled design relieved with pen slashes where he had started a clogged nib; and I knew that the workbooks were full of pinch-penned words that scrawled toward the horizon, an ever-receding horizon of expression. Here he sat every morning in his un-cozy work chair, his back to the street, his head cocked to the papers beside the typewriter, his near-sighted bespectacled eyes peering at far-sighted literature. The generous Victorian windows afforded a glimpse of St Mark's Place crossing busy First Avenue, where ethnic shoppers milled along with American bohemians from one ethnic emporium to another.

Such slovenliness is contradicted by reports of Auden's efficient running of the brownstone walk-up at 7 Middagh Street, Brooklyn Heights, which he had inhabited in the early 1940s with a host of artists and minor celebrities, including Carson McCullers and the stripper Gypsy Rose Lee. According to Brooke Allen, reviewing Sherill Tippins's account (2004) of what came to be called the 'February House,' because so many of its occupants had birthdays in this month,

> An ungainly looking mock-Tudor brownstone, it had back windows giving the same views of New York Harbor and the Brooklyn Bridge that had inspired Walt Whitman and Hart Crane. Its prox-imity to the Brooklyn Naval Yard with its collection of sailors and shipbuilders was an added attraction. ... The house was poised ... 'between bourgeois comfort and a district that boasted some of the city's most unashamed debauchery' – in other words, it was perfect.

The reputation of Auden as 'famous slob' here gave way to that of the
martinet:

> in this crowd he passed for a bourgeois, and he determined that
> regular meals and working hours be imposed ... [H]e took over,
> writing up cooking and cleaning schedules and haranguing his
> housemates when they used too much toilet paper. 'We've got a roast
> and two veg, salad and savory,' he would announce before dinner,
> 'and there will be no political discussion.' (Allen 2005)

'No one was ever less of a Bohemian,' wrote Auden's brother-in-
law, Golo Mann, dismissing the idea that the February House was a
'commune':

> [W]hen I think of the house ... the only figure I really see is Auden
> – though in the role, not of a poet of genius, but of a stern head of a
> family. There were two coloured servants, who cleaned and cooked
> the meals – formal, heavy meals which were eaten in a gloomy base-
> ment with plush-covered furniture. If anyone was late, Auden did
> not conceal his disapproval. Expenses were covered in accordance
> with a complicated system thought out by Auden; all subscribed to
> the general domestic economy, and there were individual prices for
> each meal. It was a serious question how many meals anyone had
> missed, after due notification in advance. Once a week there was a
> 'bill-day', announced with a certain satisfaction by Auden at break-
> fast time; afterwards he went from room to room collecting payment.
> ('A Memoir,' Spender 1975, 101)

Mann adds that the Austrian cottage likewise was 'meagrely furnished,'
with 'a large rough-hewn table for writing on' in the living-room, and
a couple of chairs, no bookshelves, and the floor 'covered with piles
of books and half-empty wine bottles. But this was only the outward
appearance.'

In the 'Thanksgiving for a Habitat' sequence, which describes every
room in the Kirchstetten house, Auden insisted, against all this testimony, that whereas 'Spotless rooms / where nothing's left lying about
/ chill me, so do cups used for ashtrays or smeared / with lipstick.' The
homes he warms to, he says, convey a sense of bills being promptly
settled with cheques that don't bounce. The same sequence emphasizes
the bourgeois tidiness and efficient provision in the guest bedroom, 'In
a house backed by orderly woods' (Auden 1966, 46, 37). Thekla Clark
describes fully various rooms in the *Audenhaus*, disclosing among other

things that Auden's beloved *OED* could serve a more prosaic function than lexical stimulus: one volume was always placed on the chair at the head of the dining table for him to sit on (Clark 1995, 47–8). She does not appear to have been much persuaded by the poetry's claims about tidiness:

> Keeping the house in order was a thankless task. Since the house-keeper didn't know which books and papers could be touched, nothing was ever tidied up or put away. When we arrived, I would have a session with Chester putting things away, and even throwing out old newspapers – the unfinished crosswords had been kept in the hope that someone would finish them. (As a matter of principle the answers in the next day's paper were not checked unless all the spaces had been filled in.) (Clark 1995, 62)

If, in Golo Mann's words, Auden 'attached no value to the display of possessions, but much to a strictly conducted rule of life' (Spender 1975, 101), there were selfishly practical reasons for such a Teutonically patriarchal regimen:

> 'Sit down to your writing every morning from nine to twelve for thirty years and you're bound to accomplish something,' advised Wystan, quoting his father-in-law, Thomas Mann. And Wystan did sit down to his writing every morning, from eight to one, with clock-work regularity, in the autumn of 1941. He liked the neighbourhood; and he had no hangups about his work time, about being interrupted by telephone, doorbell, mailman, or caller with legitimate business, but he would be brief with any such interruption. (Miller 1989, 22)

Thus Charles Miller, writing of the house they shared in 1940–41. The clerkly routines of Gubbins at a desk have to be kept up. Still, there's no call for unmannerly vexation with persons from Porlock. Like the poet, they're only doing their job. And they give him an occasion now and again to get up from his chair.

Works Cited

Allen, Brooke, 2005. 'The House on Middagh Street,' *The New Criterion*, 23.10 (June 2005): 74.
Auden, W. H., 1940. *Another Time*. London: Faber & Faber.
Auden, W. H., 1966. *About the House*. London: Faber & Faber.

Auden, W. H., 1975. *The Dyer's Hand*. London: Faber & Faber.

Auden, W. H., and Louis MacNeice, 1937. *Letters from Iceland*. London: Faber & Faber.

Beckett, Samuel, 1979. *The Beckett Trilogy*. London: Picador.

Bell, Kathleen, 1993. 'Nancy Spender's Recollections of Wystan Auden,' *The W. H. Auden Society Newsletter*, 10–11 (1993): 1–3.

Carpenter, Humphrey, 1981. *W. H. Auden: A Biography*. London: Allen & Unwin.

Clark, Thekla, 1995. *Wystan and Chester*. London: Faber & Faber.

Coleridge, Samuel Taylor, 1963. *Poems*, ed. John Beer. London: Dent.

Dickinson, Peter, 2001. 'Setting Auden to Music,' *The W. H. Auden Society Newsletter*, 21 (2001): 21–30.

Green, Martin, 1992. *Children of the Sun*. London: Pimlico.

Hanly, Jane, 1995. 'Jane Hanly Remembers,' *The W. H. Auden Society Newsletter*, 13 (1995): 1–5.

Isherwood, Christopher, 1937. 'Some Notes on Auden's Early Poetry,' *New Verse*, 26–27 (1937): 4–9.

Jenkins, Nicholas, 2005. 'Vin Ordinaire,' *The W.H. Auden Society Newsletter*, 25 (2005): 18–23.

Logue, Christopher, 1999. *Prince Charming: A Memoir*. London: Faber & Faber.

MacNeice, Louis, 1982. *The Strings Are False*. London: Faber & Faber.

Madge, Charles, 1937. 'Oxford Collective Poem,' *New Verse*, 25 (1937): 16–19.

Miller, Charles H., 1989. *Auden: An American Friendship*. New York: Paragon.

Norse, Harold, 1990. *Memoirs of a Bastard Angel*. London: Bloomsbury.

Rowse, A. L., 1987. *The Poet Auden: A Personal Memoir*. London: Methuen.

Smith, Stan, 2009. 'Poetry Then,' in Peter Brooker and Andrew Thacker, eds, *The Oxford Critical and Cultural History of Modernist Magazines*, Vol. I, *Britain and Ireland 1880–1955*. Oxford: Oxford University Press.

Spender, Stephen, 1951. *World Within World*. London: Hamish Hamilton.

Spender, Stephen, ed., 1975. *W. H. Auden: A Tribute*. London: Weidenfeld & Nicolson.

Sutherland, John, 2005. *Stephen Spender: The Authorized Biography*. London: Penguin.

Timpanaro, Sebastiano, 1975. 'The Freudian Slip,' *New Left Review*, 1 (1975): 91.

Tippins, Sherill, 2004. *February House: The Story of W. H. Auden, Carson McCullers, Jane & Paul Bowles, Benjamin Britten & Gypsy Rose Lee, Under One Roof in Wartime America*. New York: Houghton Mifflin.

Literary Limelight: the Laureateship

GRAEME HARPER interviews ANDREW MOTION

GH: If somebody says to you that they'd like to talk about your 'creative environment,' what are your immediate thoughts?

AM: What do you mean, 'creative environment'? That's my first question. Do you mean my life, or how I arrange things so I can get some writing done?

GH: Both!

AM: I've always thought it would be good for me to lead my life in a way which was very closely connected with my work, and at the same time to clear spaces where work can happen. But it's not easy, because my life is very busy, which makes it difficult to find long stretches when I can sit at my desk, and even more difficult to find times when I can stare into space and cogitate.

By last autumn [2007], I'd got myself into the situation of hardly writing anything at all. I hadn't written a poem – apart from when my father died eighteen months previously – for about three years. I'd never had such a long time without writing before in my life. It was largely due to being busy: always sitting on trains, always having to go, always visiting schools, always doing this, always doing that, sitting in meetings of one kind or another. I don't say this in a complaining spirit. It's simply an observation of how my life had become. I'd made a bed and I was lying in it.

In combination with these practical pressures, there are peculiar pressures for anyone doing the job of Poet Laureate. They made me wary of myself. Wary of risking failure. I felt that there were too many people looking at me, and waiting for me to fall flat on my face. So that had a pretty silencing effect. Then, last winter, as a result of various upheavals in my personal life, and a deliberate rearrangement of my day in order to make time to write, I began writing again. In fact in the last three or four months I've written more poems than I would normally expect to write in about three years. They were still there, the poems; it was just a question of getting at them.

What this has meant, in practical terms, is being very strict with myself. I make myself get up a little bit earlier than I used to do. These days, come ten o'clock, I've had three hours at my desk, which means I don't especially mind what happens to the rest of the day. I can go and teach. I can write journalism. I can do my work for the Poetry Archive or the Museums, Libraries and Archives Council (of which I'm chair). I can go and make visits, or I can go to the library. Provided I'm able to move from my bed to my desk carrying this about-to-overflow-bucket-of-poetry without spilling anything, then I'm okay.

So it comes down to this. I feel my poems must be part of life. But if life turns out to be too busy, then I have to make deliberate efforts to create a sort of artificial environment for them to begin. Perhaps I shouldn't say that: I just don't know what other people's circumstances are like. It'll be interesting to see what happens when I stop being Laureate. More and more different kinds of writing, I hope.

GH: Could you say more about the relation between a public role and writing?

AM: There's something I left out of my account of what seems to have been going on when I'd stopped writing. And it's this. I'd become bored with my own poems. I don't mean that I'd become terminally fed up with the ones I'd already written. What I'd become bored with was being able to predict, quite accurately, what a poem was going to end up looking like as I started it. I think that, again, was partly a Laureate-ship problem. I needed to work out how to reroute myself, how to find a slightly different voice, and it took me a long time to do it. The whole process was very complicatedly bound up with the sorts of freedoms which eventually made themselves felt after my father died.

My readers know I've written a lot about my mother, and as a result probably think of me as an Oedipal kind of writer. With good reason: what happened to her was overwhelmingly traumatic. But my father also exerted an enormous influence on me – partly because he was the parent left standing, but partly because he was a powerful personality, in his comparatively silent way. He wasn't a tyrant, not by any means, but I did feel very obliged to him. Now he's not there to oblige.

Anyway, for several reasons it took me quite a long time to find this new voice I wanted – something much more relaxed, funnier when it needed to be, sadder too, plainer, more worldly. Previously I'd been preoccupied by writing in tighter and tighter forms, and I now just wanted to loosen them all. Maybe they'll all come back one day, these strictnesses, but at the moment I'm very pleased not to feel – I use the same word again, interestingly – *obliged*. I'm happy to be writing more freely.

GH: This notion of 'fallow,' the 'building up' period is intriguing.

AM: Yes, it turned out to be a building-up, thank God! At the time I'd never felt such a blow to my sense of my self, particularly since it coincided with me spending a lot of time trotting round the country talking about poetry. It was a strange paradox.

GH: A non-Poet Laureate!

AM: Quite! I felt very troubled by it. I can remember Larkin talking about stopping writing and saying 'it's a sorrow, but not a crushing sorrow.' But it was getting pretty close to being a crushing sorrow in my case. I'm sure he (Larkin) didn't feel he'd said all he wanted to say, but he certainly had a very secure sense of merit and value in what he had done. I've never had that. I felt, 'I've only just started, and then I've stopped,' or I appeared to have stopped.

GH: Did you find yourself trying to come up with tricks to kick-start yourself?

AM: Yes, but, of course, they don't really work. And as the poems receded from me, as the whole business of sitting down to write became more and more problematic, it also became, as a sort of defence mechanism, less appealing. Reading other people's poems became less attractive to me as well. So I stopped liking a lot of poems.

GH: How did you do your work in schools, then? Obviously, your public role didn't go away.

AM: Well, I kept up a good front. I was polite about it – without being insincere.

GH: What's your advocacy for the writing arts based on?

AM: My earliest adult experience of poetry, which came when my English teacher at school made me read poems for the first time, and made them feel absolutely part of life, but at the same time full of mystery. They move at different speeds from most of the other things in life. More slowly. They concentrate the mind in a way that few other things do. As poets, we shouldn't cosset ourselves in ivory towers but get out there, read the paper, sit on a bus, be normal, be in there among the stuff; but we should also be star-gazers.

GH: Having said that, when you first were talking about getting into a pattern of being able to work you referred to your desk three or four times. So there's a specific physical space and there is a specific physical action?

AM: There is and, in a narrow sense, that is my environment. My partner and I live in a small flat off the Camden Road [in north London]. We complain a bit, because it really is pretty tiny, but we like it, and it has the advantage of making me think of my study as a kind of capsule for writing in. That's how I feel about it, my room. There's nothing special about it. It's just a small room, full of books, where poems happen. That's the idea, anyway. And at the moment, thank God, it seems to be working like that.

GH: Do you drag poems kicking and screaming into the room, or do you find them in there?

AM: At the moment, some of them begin in the room and some of them begin outside the room. But they all get finished in the room. They don't all work, of course, but …

GH: So you discard a lot?

AM: I discard about four times as much as I keep. I've always done that. I've always written much, much, much more than I keep. Sometimes I come back to the same idea later, and treat it in a different way, but, by and large, if it goes wrong, that's it. The routine of working goes something like this. I wake up early in the morning and start thinking about poems before I get up. If I get up at half six, or something like that, I've usually already had at least an hour of thinking about poems – thinking in that floating, suggestible state that's so conducive to writing, just listening to early traffic going past, the birds waking up, and all that kind of thing. And listening to quietness. That's when I feel close to sharing that thing Frost talks about – how poems begin with a lump in the throat, a love-sickness, a home-sickness.

That's to say: my poems in most cases begin as intense, but non-verbal, events. They're much more like music or pure sensation than they are like the word on the page that they are destined to become. As this sort of yearning, longing feeling makes itself manifest, then my conscious brain gets to work on it, and starts to manipulate and interrogate and test, and sees what sort of equivalent the feeling has in an act of saying or writing. At that point, the emerging poem moves into the slightly better-lit front of our mind, which is where all the readerly, writerly, wired-up, and on-the-case bits of my mind start to grapple with it. Quite a lot of the negotiation between conscious and unconscious mind has happened before I am even aware of what the subject is. And then the subject becomes evident, or the situation becomes evident – it might be something in memory, it might be something that happened yesterday, it might be something from childhood, it might be (and very often is for me) something that I've read in a book – something that has achieved an equivalent status to actual life by being pondered and enjoyed. Then I go through to my study and I start writing it down. Usually the first several phrases will have already occurred to me by that time. So drafting a poem, or beginning to draft a poem, which looks like the beginning of a process, is in fact quite a long way down the track.

For instance, the other week I was reading Richard Fortey's new book about the Natural History Museum, *Dry Store Room No. 1: The Secret Life of the Natural History Museum*. I read a lot of natural history books, partly for enjoyment, partly as a manifestation of green-ery, partly because it's a way of connecting myself with a country childhood. He has a story about a man who, I think, was in palaeontology when Fortey began working at the museum himself. The then keeper of the museum was incredibly pleased to have appointed this man, Bairstow, who was the youngest Fellow there had ever been at King's, Cambridge, and a real whiz with his subject, which was belemnites, very dull-looking fossils. There were a lot of them up by Whitby so he was going to publish a fantastic study of this fossil, and was always nipping up to Whitby, and spending hours combing through the layers of the River Esk, that runs into the sea there. But the years went by and he never published anything, and gradually his study became more and more like a sort of spider's web-*cum*-labyrinth-*cum*-maze. Eventually he retired, having never published a word, and they cleared out his room after he'd left the building. He'd become pre-emptively perfectionist in his cataloguing of things. They found some shoeboxes in which he'd been storing bits of string. One of the shoeboxes said 'two to three foot long,' one of them said 'one to two foot long,' and one of them said 'too small to be of any use.' I thought this was absolutely wonderful. I lived with the story in my head so vividly, I almost felt I'd been clearing out the room myself. In that way things in books do become part of life – another, felt life, an actual life.

Does that make me sound bookish? So be it. Most of the poets that have meant most to me, particularly Wordsworth and Edward Thomas, are writers who appear to be as natural as the day they were born, and un-literary. On closer inspection, they turn out to be little echo chambers of other people's words, either actually alluding to them or, more often, simmering with the language of other, sympathetic writers. It's William Hazlitt's idea of the 'cento' [a network of sounding phrases from other authors]. So I've always tried to write poems that looked completely natural, but which I'm well aware are full of previous poems.

GH: What occurs then, in terms of redrafting or rethinking?

AM: Once I've got a poem down on paper, more or less, from beginning to end, I'll tinker with it on that same day, and then I'll let it stand, as though it was something that I've taken out of the oven. Then, over the next several days, I'll tinker with it a bit more. Then I'll put it away, and probably bring it out again in a month's time, or something like that, and give it another going over. It is very difficult to get a proper degree of dispassion in the revising process. Poems have got to become strange to us, and part of us has got to become almost indifferent to them before we can see them as clearly as we must. We've got to stop feeling protective of them, and of the 'suffering,' in quote marks, that got them written in the first place, so that we can be completely hard-nosed in our later approaches to them. I've found that changing the typeface helps, getting it out of the handwritten onto the screen. But I also find that if a poem comes out in a magazine or newspaper before it gets put in a book, which usually happens, that's a very interesting distancing moment. The poem starts to look as if it's been written by somebody else then, and that allows the sort of toughness that you need.

GH: You never do something at your desk and immediately run out screaming 'Look at this! Look what I've finished!'

AM: No! Always revision. I was never a creative writing student, and it would have been difficult for me to be one, being the age that I am, unless I'd gone to America. But luckily, ever since my late teens, I've had a person to show my poems to: Alan Hollinghurst, with whom I used to share a house as a student. He's my best friend, and of course a wonderful writer. Before our books get sent off to the publishers, we always show each other our stuff – critically. I've got a new book coming out next spring, and it's just come back from Alan. We've had a day talking about it. Poems disappear and verses get rewritten and orders get changed – really fundamental things. And when he's about to publish a book I, along with other people, see what he's doing. What goes on in those conversations is a model for what should happen in creative writing workshops. It's very supportive: the assumption is that we like what each other is doing, but the comments are very tough. Tough, but sort of kindly put.

GH: Do you have a circle of friends who are writers, and then an alternate or concentric circle of non-writer friends? Who do you tend to bounce things off?

AM: My partner, who I live with, is not a literary person, and she'd be the first to say so. She is Korean. Her English is very good and she lived in America for a long time before we met, but she's not a bookworm. She knows a lot about language – she's a translator and an interpreter – and, of course, I share with her the things I write, particularly if she's involved in them, which she often is. But she doesn't offer much in the way of detailed criticism. We don't spend much time talking about that sort of stuff at home, which is how we both like it. Of the half dozen or so friends that I have, most of them are writers of one kind or another – though none of my close friends write poems. There's a sort of circle outside that are poets. I'm friendly with a lot of poets, but not close. Well, I feel myself to be friendly with a lot of poets. I hope they'd say the same!

GH: One of the interesting notions floating around is that creative writers are always writing, even if they are not pen in hand or even discussing writing. Is this a fundamental part of a creative writer's landscape?

AM: I see myself in some sense as an *occasional* poet. I don't mean that usually I only write occasionally or only write for formal occasions, but that everything in life is an occasion that I might write a poem about. But I've never wanted to be the kind of poet who goes swanning around with the back of his hand pressed to his forehead saying 'I'm a poet, I'm a poet,' and waiting to be hit by a bolt of lightning. One of the nicest things that's ever been said to me was by the guy who worked in the lodge at my college at university [Motion was at Oxford]. He was called Douglas, he was getting on, and he'd seen it all. On my last day at college, I went to say goodbye to him and to thank him, and he said, 'Well, I will say this to you, Mr Motion, for a bloody poet you've got your feet on the ground.' I thought that was terrific.

GH: And yet …

AM: Yes – in the same breath I want to insist there is mystery in poems. The poems we love, we love partly because they always exist at a point just beyond our full understanding. So all this practicality and get-on-with-it-ness is not there to make poetry simply plain bread and cheese. It's just to make sure that it's – as I keep saying – absolutely part of life.

GH: Can I ask you about your biographical sense, a professional closeness to other writers, a sense of what other writers do?

AM: I've always thought one should be at liberty to say there are writers one just doesn't like. You might think they're quite good, but your brain isn't tuned to them. There aren't many of those. Then there's quite a big group of people that you like, and would certainly read if you found a book of theirs sitting by your bed. Then there are a few writers you think the world of. And then there are half a dozen, if that, that you're in love with. It's not that you won't hear a word against them, it's that even the words against them make them sound fascinating – Edward Thomas, Wilfred Owen, Shakespeare. Those are three of my half dozen. Wordsworth; he's another. When I've got a problem to solve in a poem, I ask myself: what would they have done? Or what they did do, indeed.

GH: Are they sitting around your desk?

AM: They're in reach, all the time, though the ones I really love are sort of 'off by heart', in that good phrase. And this is a good way of speaking about 'the environment,' as you did at the beginning. It turns out to be an interesting, rich concept, this, doesn't it? I'd started not quite knowing what it meant. Now I have lots of senses of what it might mean. In addition to the writers I have as friends, and what I happen to be reading, it means that I keep a sort of ghostly company as well. They say quite simple things actually, these ghosts, simple but necessary: 'Keep going,' 'Don't worry too much about the short-term questions of reputation' ... and 'Never be complacent.'

There are novelists and poets whose work has deteriorated because the flame of their talent has died down, which of course can happen, and is not entirely in a person's control. But there are also writers who make the mistake of starting to think that what they do is top-notch. That's the beginning of the end. We all have to keep remembering the famous Beckett thing, about failing better all the time. We have to retain a proper degree of modesty, in the face of the subject, and admit to our disappointment in what we manage to do. There's nothing so likely to make us get out of bed the next morning and have another crack at it.

GH: And in your fallow period?

AM: Well, some days I thought, 'It's gone, it's gone. It left Philip Larkin, why shouldn't it leave me? I could have done so much better.' There were so many other things I wanted to write about. Then other days I thought, 'Well, better to be writing nothing than writing crap.' I remembered Louis MacNeice, a poet I like very much, and how he went on publishing through his quite long, less-than-best time. Eventually his genius came back, and his last book is his best book. I told myself, 'Either stay silent and bide your time, or privately scribble things and watch them fail. But somehow or other stay vigilant, because it might come back.' In the end I climbed my way out of it, by making myself write. Not with a view to publication. Not with a view to showing the poems to anybody. Just by getting my confidence back, and by trying to develop a slightly different way of writing.

GH: You wouldn't have predicted that, after many years, something evolutionary would occur?

AM: I've always thought my poems might go away. I've always thought being a writer is like being a tree; the bird of poetry might land in you, but it might fly away again. I'm very, very happy to be back, I mean it's ... I'm very happy. Who knows how much this unblocking has got to do with the fact that I've only got a year to go as Laureate?

GH: You'll still be doing your school visits, I'm sure.

AM: I hope so. I'd be sorry if some of the things I've got interested in while I've been Laureate didn't stay with me in some way. I've spent so much time, for instance, sitting in committee rooms bullying the government about education policy and thinking about what happens on the National Curriculum, nagging about literary archives. I really want to go on being involved in those sorts of things.

I felt that the post of Laureate needed revising, in a respectful way. I've tried to do that, both on the writing side of the job and pretty much inventing the doing side to the job. If I can find a way of continuing those things without getting in the way of my successor then I'd be very pleased to do that.

A Bed of One's Own: Margaret Oliphant

ELISABETH JAY

THE HALF-CENTURY SPAN of Oliphant's writing career witnessed extraordinary transformations to the world she wrote in, about, and for. In one of her last articles for *Blackwood's Magazine*, "'Tis Sixty years Since,' she used the occasion of Queen Victoria's Diamond Jubilee to outline some of these, drawing particular attention to means of travel, swifter communication, medical advances, the growth in philanthropy, and changes in fashion. In her own lifetime, she noted, canals had given way to railways, people had become habituated to the new 'magic slaves' of the paddle steamer and telegram, India had become a tourist destination rather than a far-flung outpost of Empire; the postal system had been revolutionized, and the provinces had acquired daily newspapers (Oliphant 1897b). Many of these developments had a direct impact upon her life as a writer. She could pop up to London for the day from Windsor, where she spent thirty years of her career, without losing an evening's writing; her proofs could be turned around swiftly; she found a new outlet for her work in the daily papers. She became an intrepid traveller. Not relishing sea travel, she never undertook the trip to America that many of her contemporaries made, but, in 1890, she extended her many journeys to Europe to embrace the Holy Land. These foreign experiences informed her fiction and inspired her series of historical guides to various European cities. Only two months before her death in 1897, while suffering from cancer of the colon, she undertook a three-week trip to Siena to research a further book in this series.

However, there were important elements of continuity across a long writing life, begun at age seventeen at 22 Juvenal Street, Everton, Liverpool in 1845. For one thing, although she used others to write letters on her behalf, she never took to dictation to a stenographer, as Henry James so notably did. She continued to write her first drafts by hand, complaining to her publisher in her sixty-sixth year that 'I have worked a little hole in my right forefinger – with the pen, I suppose! – and can't get it to heal, – also from excessive use of that little implement' (Oliphant 1974, 426).

Her first work, the novel *Christian Melville* (1856), which she was later to dismiss as a 'very silly' piece of juvenilia (Oliphant 2002, 60), established other patterns that would characterize her creative practices over the next half century. Depressed by her own part in the breakdown of her first engagement, and condemned to silence by her sick mother's need for absolute quiet, the daughter wiled away hours of bedside-nursing in a mental distraction that fed off her familial preoccupations. A prefatory sonnet, exalting domestic sainthood above other forms of goodness, is suggestive of the place that personal circumstance would so often play in Oliphant's fiction: 'But fairer still, mid quiet household life, / A calm sad chastened spirit praising Thee' (Oliphant 1856, title page). 'The chief character' in this fiction, she subsequently recalled, had been 'an angelic elder sister, unmarried, who had the charge of a family of motherless brothers and sisters, and who had a shrine of sorrow in her life in the shape of the portrait and memory of her lover who had died young' (Oliphant 2002, 60). The protected youngest child's yearning for a larger field in which to assume self-denying responsibilities was to be amply fulfilled in later life. When her husband died, in 1859, leaving her alone in Italy with two young children, pregnant, and £1000 in debt, Oliphant took charge of a family which over time grew to include her eldest brother, three of his children, an alcoholic middle brother, and a distant cousin. This extended family became the justification for a career that eventually produced some ninety-eight novels, fifty or more short stories, twenty-five works of non-fiction, and over three hundred reviews and essays.

Yet her family, as she well knew, was not her first motive: the constant writing, spilling over from books and articles, into thousands of letters, and intermittent diary-keeping, was an addiction. 'I have written because it gave me pleasure, because it came natural to me, because it was like talking or breathing, besides the big fact that it was necessary for me to work for my children,' she wrote in her autobiography (Oliphant 2002, 48). In 1863 she told her publisher that 'the disease is got to be chronic with me, and I must work or die; not to speak of the daily – nay, hourly – necessity of bread and butter' (Oliphant 1974, 192).

Interestingly, given the self-medicating cocktails (often including opium) which sustained many of her contemporaries, Oliphant found her own robust health and 'criminally elastic' temperament in the face of so many family tragedies almost culpable. Her autobiography recorded, as a memorable exception, the occasion some thirty years earlier when 'terrified,' because of her pregnancy, that she would be unable to nurse her dying husband 'to the last,' she had taken a dose of laudanum. She could not remember whether this had been self-prescribed or given by a doctor, but she recalled effects that she presumably subsequently decided were incompatible with either adequate mothering or creativity: 'I recollect very well the sudden floating into ease of body and the dazed condition of mind, – a kind of exaltation, as if I were walking upon air, for I could not sleep in the circumstances nor try to sleep. I thought then that this was the saving of me' (Oliphant 2002, 182, 120).

In 1894, towards the end of her life, when both of the sons who had survived to adulthood were dead, she found herself, once again, needing to rationalize the nature of the personal gratification that her creativity had provided:

> I have always been most grateful to God that it was work I liked and that interested me in the doing of it, and it has often carried me away from myself and quenched, or at least calmed, the troubles of life. ... [M]y own stories, in the making of them were very much what other people's stories (but these the very best) were in the reading ... But this does not mean that I was indifferent to the work as work, or did not beat it out with interest and pleasure. It pleases me at this present moment, I may confess, that I seem to have found unawares an image that quite expresses what I mean – *i.e.*, that I wrote as I read, with much the same sort of feeling. It seems to me that this is rather an original way of putting it (to disclose the privatest thought of my mind), and this gives me an absurd little sense of pleasure. (Oliphant 2002, 164)

This passage, pondering her own creativity, is remarkable both for its insights and its blindspots. Its overt engagement with Christian duty exists alongside mingled pride and self-ridicule in contemplating her own achievements, and a sense of the filters the creative mind applies in contemplating its own processes. A Carlylean doctrine of the spiritual value of labour is hitched, apparently effortlessly, to a conceit of the imagination as escapist or narcotic. It would have astonished George Eliot's Maggie Tulliver, as she fought against fiction's power to distract from everyday concerns, or the Tennyson of *In Memoriam*, who recognized craftsmanship's ability to numb pain. Daydreaming, or 'fantasticating' (the word Oliphant sometimes used to describe her story-making), is here given a positive charge by imaging it as physically demanding labour that 'beats out' its products. In this way the plotting of fictions that were often extrapolated from immediate domestic predicaments to form imagined alternative outcomes, could be allied to practical and energetic scheming for one's family.

Mid-nineteenth-century creative writing was like a cottage industry, in that it took the form of piece-work practised at home, at a time when the national trend was towards centralization and mechanization. Male authors frequently expressed anxieties about appearing to be feminized by the domestic setting of their work. They also felt the danger of being classed with manual labourers, rather than with gentlemen whose status depended upon having little visible engagement with the creation of their own wealth. Women writers, however, often learned to profit from the ambiguities of their position. Writing provided a sense of purpose and a channel for the energy which the constraining ideology of early Victorian middle-class gentility threatened to sap. It could also be made to offer *visible* evidence of a woman's willingness to work for her family, which the increasing division of labour, male from female and servant's from mistress's, was obscuring.

Silent self-sacrifice was the ideal to which women of Oliphant's generation were taught to aspire. Also the pretence, at least, of relying on their menfolk for support, partly distinguished middle-class women from their working-class sisters, who could not afford to be maintained inviolate from the moral compromises and rough practicalities of the marketplace. Just as many manuals of domestic etiquette and household management of the day can now be seen as prescriptive rather than descriptive, so, with hindsight, one can see women writers, more or less consciously, shaping their individual creative environments into conformity with these precepts. It is the similarity with which women from different backgrounds describe their writing practice that reveals the sway of an almost universal cultural imperative operating at the very moment of creation where one might have anticipated the maximum divergence. Thus, Elizabeth Gaskell, an urban, Unitarian minister's wife, writing in her dining-room, exposed to a flow of domestic activity and queries, and Charlotte Yonge, a wealthy, rural Anglican spinster, instantly replacing her ailing mother's needs by those of a crippled younger relative, were both making the same statement: their writing was congruent with their domestic duties. Oliphant's mother spelt out the same message in the sparser surroundings of their Liverpool terraced house.

[T]he writing ran through everything. But then it was also subor- dinate to everything, to be pushed aside for any little necessity. I had no table even to myself, much less a room to work in, but sat at the corner of the family table with my writing book, with every- thing going on as if I had been making a shirt instead of writing a book. Our rooms were in those days sadly wanting in artistic arrangement. The table was in the middle of the room, the centre round which everybody sat with the candles or lamp upon it. My mother sat always at needlework of some kind, and talked to whoever might be present, and I took my share in the conversation, going on all the same with my story, the little groups of imaginary persons, these other talks evolving themselves quite undisturbed. It would put me out now to have some one sitting at the same table talking while I worked – at least I say I would think it put me out, with that sort of conventionalism which grows upon one. But up to this date, 1888, I have never been shut up in a separate room or hedged off with any observances. My study, all the study I have ever attained to, is the little second drawing-room of my house with a wide opening into the other drawing-room where all the (feminine) life of the house goes on; and I don't think that I have ever had two hours undisturbed (except at night, when everybody is in bed) during my whole literary life ... I think the first time I ever secluded myself for my work was years after it had become my profession and sole dependence – when I was living in my widowhood in a relation's house and withdrew my book and my inkstand from the family drawing-room out of a little conscious ill-temper which made me feel guilty notwithstanding that the retirement was so very justifiable! But I did not feel it to be so, neither did the companions from whom I withdrew! (Oliphant 2002, 66–7)

Her mother's arrangements, intended to prevent any sense of exceptionality, or alienating precocity, in her daughter's accomplishments, became important in more significant ways for the kind of writer Oliphant became. It allowed her to move easily back and forth between characters' inner thoughts and the way in which they were perceived by their family, friends, and neighbours. This was particularly useful in providing a salutary antidote to passages of thinly disguised self-pity. Her ability to feed off the events and feelings of her own life but also to stand back and see herself as overbearing, self-martyring, and occasionally ridiculous bears comparison with that of James Joyce. His upbringing in straitened and physically claustrophobic family circumstances seems to have taught him a similar capacity for subjecting this compulsive interest in the minutiae of his own life to mocking scrutiny.

The basic furniture and absence of 'artistic arrangement' in her formative creative environment also played their role in Oliphant's formation as a writer. On the one hand this convinced her of the simplicity of the writer's needs: a source of light and a supply of ink. The absence of ritualistic procedures, talismanic objects, or specially contrived places

Plate 1: Margaret Oliphant's drawing room and study in Windsor.

meant that she could, and did, write undistractedly wherever she found herself. In a passage of her autobiography written in 1891 she mentions still possessing her husband's 'touching' painting, 'The Prodigal,' but without any sense of its being more than a pleasing keepsake. During her marriage and early widowhood Oliphant could not afford the luxury of an obsession with a particular location, desk or objet d'art, moving as she frequently did from one rented property to another. Location seems not to have been problematic for her writing: her powers of recall were such that she was able to continue an English or Scottish tale in a European spa town and to recreate what she required of foreign environments back in England. Anne Thackeray Ritchie vouched for the almost parsimonious equipment employed by this fellow writer whom she first met in Grindelwald:

> I used to see her at her daily task, steadily continuing, notwithstanding all the interruptions of nature and human nature – the changing lights on the mountains, the many temptations to leave her task. I was always struck, when I saw her writing, by her concentration and the perfect neatness of her arrangements – the tiny inkstand of prepared ink into which she poured a few drops of water, enough for each day's work the orderly manuscript, her delicate, fine pen. (Ritchie 1913, 22–3)

On the other hand the simple furnishings of her childhood home made her particularly aware of the bric-à-brac accumulated in wealthier Victorian homes as a fine gauge of status and temperament. The picture of her Windsor study, and the cluttered drawing-room it gives onto (Plate 1), show how she herself joined the acquisitive classes. Nevertheless, her fiction retained a sharp eye for the material ways in which her characters expressed themselves. She had nothing but contempt for male bibelot-hunters, frittering time and money away on non-essentials, or for the displays of the *nouveaux riches*, but she demonstrated real understanding for the significance women often seemed to attach to the redesign of a garden, or the laying of new carpet, as symptoms of their ability to impose something of themselves in a world whose material circumstances were almost wholly controlled by male earning power or inherited wealth. Her novel, *Phoebe Junior* (1876), featuring a heroine who sees marriage as a route to a career rather than as the culmination of a grand passion, could be seen as offering a reflective commentary on the role played by material comfort in the creative life. Phoebe has made the most of a metropolitan upbringing, and learned that less is always more in matters of tasteful display: this lesson stands her in good stead when she finds herself reduced to more meagre aesthetic surroundings in a provincial county town. Faced with the task of mounting an impromptu tea-party for two urbane young men, in the relentlessly working-class surroundings of her grandparents' home, she proves extraordinarily resourceful. Instead of despising a small cottage piano as an inadequate instrument for displaying her considerable skills, she charms her audience with her truly accomplished playing; and, in the absence of *objets d'art*, draws attention to the fine cream Wedgwood tea-service that her unsophisticated grandmother employs for everyday use, on the grounds that it is older than the fashionable china she has since purchased. The index of Phoebe's creativity is her capacity to work with the humblest of materials, and the reader learns to esteem it in comparison with the practical incompetence of other girls of her own age, and the bitterness of aristocratic spinsters whose decorative instincts are forever destined to be thwarted by allusion to the likes and dislikes of the heir and his wife.

The sense of domestic space as gendered, instilled since the earliest days, when her mother commanded the social life of the family table while her father remained a shadowy, unsociable figure, was also to prove significant for her writing. First, it influenced the content and style of her work. Although she experimented, early in her career especially, with different fictional genres, her best-loved novels exploit familial relationships and tensions, often pitting men's freedom to retreat, without explanation, to exclusively male spaces – be it a working men's club, the library, or a smoking room – against women's exposure to the unremitting surveillance of family, servants, and visitors. In Oliphant's writings the appeal of the library is as a protected space for reflection and writing more than as a collection of books or access to knowledge. Oliphant swiftly became adept at describing the emotions of women forced to keep up the pretence of sociability whilst their inner thoughts ranged in directions often at odds with the guarded composure of their spoken observations.

Her work, in that it was undertaken from the first under a social gaze, was always written with a sense of audience. If a woman's musical ability could be justified, in more privileged families, by its capacity to provide family entertainment, so could writing, if it could be reconfig-ured as providing amusement for the domestic circle. Unlike Charles Dickens, who found his closest sense of relationship with his audience through staged public readings, many women writers seem to have benefited from an early point in their career from using immediate family members as a sounding board. Elizabeth Gaskell, presumably relying on Charlotte Brontë's testimony, had drawn the memorable picture of the Brontë sisters pacing the parsonage parlour together of an evening to 'find fault or to sympathise' with the accounts of each others' writing (Gaskell 1997, 300). Oliphant recalled a similar combination of support and criticism.

> I had nobody to praise me except my mother and Frank [her eldest brother] … After a while it came to be part of the custom that I should every night 'read what I had written' to them before I went to bed. They were very critical sometimes, and I felt while I was reading whether my little audience was with me or not, which put a good deal of excitement into the performance. (Oliphant 2002, 66)

This regular procedure encouraged the swift development of a sense of form and drama, leading Oliphant to arrive at the episodic length, dramatic climaxes, and the convincing dialogue that would, in turn, captivate the families where her serialized stories were read aloud. It also seems to have been influential in determining her fluent style, capable of carrying a wide range, from her characters' complex interior reflection to the narrator's mordantly witty commentary. By the mid-1890s, when she came to appraise the importance of the auditory element in her own composition, she was very aware of doing so in an era that favoured self-conscious stylists such as Walter Pater, Henry James, and Oscar Wilde.

> I always took pleasure in a little bit of fine writing (afterwards called in the family language a 'trot'), which, to do myself justice, was only done when I got moved by my subject, and began to feel my heart beat, and perhaps a little water in my eyes, and ever more really satisfied by some little conscious felicity of words than by anything else. I have always had my singsong, guided by no sort of law, but by my ear, which was in its way fastidious to the cadence and measure that pleased me; but it is bewildering to me in my perfectly artless art, if I may use the word at all, to hear of the elaborate ways of forming and enhancing style, and all the studies for that end. (Oliphant 2002, 149)

Beneath this self-effacement lies an affirmation of literature's power to move rather than dazzle, and of the desirability of rendering reading matter accessible in an age when the gap was visibly widening between highbrow and lowbrow art. Oliphant's preference for addressing the common reader, with all the diverse interests and experiences that implies, had been honed from the first by submitting her work to this trusted 'focus group' of a mother, forty years her senior, and Frank, a brother, her elder by twelve years. Their criticisms must, in any case, have sharpened her sense of her writing as work in progress, subject to daily revision. The precise points at which this practice of daily reading aloud changed over the years are not always easy to fathom. Plangent passages in later novels about the anxiety caused to mothers by undutiful sons make it seem unlikely that her own wayward brood formed part of the evening audience. However, Oliphant had been fortunate in finding an alternative, professional sounding-board, very early in her career. From 1852 when the firm of Blackwoods became her major publisher, she sustained a regular correspondence with John Blackwood, and, to a lesser extent, his successor, William, about the work she had in hand for them, sometimes agreeing to minor amendments, but more often standing her ground and robustly defending her own plots, characterization, opinions, and style. In early widowhood, when her household only comprised young children and a maid, she was even grateful for the nearly instantaneous public reaction generated by serial publication. In May 1863 she wrote to Blackwood about her novel, *The Perpetual Curate*:

> I think if it suits you, I should rather like the first part to appear next month. Though I am not sure I approve of it in theory, it seems to suit me in practice, and the publication and the talk stimulates and keeps me up. Very likely this is because I have nobody at home nowadays to talk it over with; but I think it is for the advantage of the work to be written just as it is published. (Oliphant 1974, 191)

She was astonished when she read John Cross's *George Eliot's Life as Related in her Letters and Journals* (1883) by its account of the need to protect this hypersensitive writer from adverse comments. It prompted Oliphant to question 'Should I have done any better if I had been kept like her, in a mental greenhouse and taken care of?' On reflection she decided that, although the responsibilities incurred in family life clearly impeded an artist, 'In all likelihood our minds and our circumstances are so arranged, that, after all, the possible way is the way that is best' (Oliphant 2002, 50).

Oliphant died in 1897 and her posthumous *Autobiography* appeared two years later. Her writing life had been so long that many of her obituarists and reviewers followed Oliphant's own lead in seeing her as representing an outmoded generation whose views were wholly out of sympathy with the 'new gospel of selfishness … being preached by women – self-development, self-assertion, the right to be herself, to live her own life; it is always self in some form that is set as the ideal before the young women of the day' (Sturgis 1899, 234). Nevertheless, there are important limiting qualifications slipped into Oliphant's record of the family-centred sociability of her own creative practice. The curtains between her inner sanctum and the drawing-room in Plate 1 suggest that they could have served as the practical equivalent of a 'Do not disturb' notice. Moreover, the prominence of the bookcase, the projection of the shelf of the small writing desk to the left, and the day-bed where reading and note-taking presumably occurred, could be said to put her work on display as much as absorb it into the domestic routine. And then comes that all-important parenthetic correction to her claim never to have had extended periods for solitary composition – '(except at night, when everybody is in bed).'

Howard Overing Sturgis couched his recollections in the light of his early adolescent encounters, as a boy at Eton, with the gracious presence of a famous author prepared to make time to welcome a young admirer into her home. Her intimates and contemporaries, particularly those in whose houses she had stayed, were more aware of the way in which she accomplished the illusion of being a prolific writer apparently never in need of a room of her own: 'There was no time in the day when she could not be seen. She may be said to have been always working, but her work never obtruded' (Porter 1898, 350). She was, in Henry James's words, 'a night-working spinner.' He hints at the uncanny, almost magical, quality he found in the careless profusion of the output achieved by this 'great *improvisatrice*' (James 1914, 359). For Oliphant herself, the twilight hour, which tales of the preternatural had traditionally represented as opening doors into other worlds, had long marked the beginning of her working day, or at least the hour when she began to 'fantasticate.' In adolescence her writing had had to wait until the day's chores were finished. Although establishing herself as the recognized general utility woman for Blackwoods had depended upon her being able to respond, in the midst of the chaos of a day while moving house in 1856, to a request for a review at short notice (Oliphant 1897a, II, 475), her usual pattern was to write at night.

The desire to be available to her children during the day partly determined this routine. As the years passed, servants arrived and schooling occupied more of the children's time, but her working habits did not change. An early widowhood was probably the most important factor in her night working because, through this stroke of misfortune, she achieved the undisturbed enjoyment of a room of her own – her bedroom. Wherever she was staying this retreat remained open to her. A hostess who had little liking for Oliphant (her husband had had an earlier fancy for the young widow, and she also thought herself the model for Oliphant's monstrously egotistic comic heroine, Lucilla Marjoribanks) wrote disapprovingly that, although her guest was never to be seen writing,

> after she had left us, my servants told me that she had asked for a pair of spare candles each night, and they were invariably consumed, telling of long hours of midnight toil. When the household began to be roused in the morning, her light could still be observed through the chinks of the shutters; shortly afterwards it was extinguished. She did not usually appear at breakfast. (Story 1913, 48–9)

The pursed lips characterizing the account of her guest's unseemly behaviour, penned by this thrifty wife of the manse, reward examination. First, Oliphant's strange hours cost money: the disappearing candles, for which the servants had obviously had to account, were probably made of the more expensive beeswax usually issued to guests, rather than the cheaper tallow candles and oil-lamp, which would have adorned the family table of Oliphant's parents. Furthermore, this guest would have required a coal-fire in the grate, at least in winter months. The significance of lighting in a Victorian writer's life is marked by the way in which Oliphant dwells on the subject in her retrospective article, ''Tis Sixty Years Since.' She recalled the smoky flame, 'at once feeble and wavery,' given off by the cruse of oil that formed 'a very dim aid to the fire-light on a cottage hearth.' Even in 'homes of middle-class respectability,' 'a pair of candles, flanked by a snuffer tray was considered sufficient for ordinary family purposes. Lamps came slowly.' The appalling smell given off by the new 'lucifer' matches, or the 'spunks,' as the Scots called the bunch of sticks dipped in brimstone used to ignite the reeking animal fat of the tallow candles, also remained with her. The greater illumination produced by clustering wax candles was reserved for 'gala nights, except in those ineffable houses of the great' (Oliphant 1897b, 604). It is thus a measure of the grandeur of Lucilla Marjoribanks's ambition to provide artistic direction for her local community when, on her first night home, she lights 'all the candles in the large old-fashioned candlesticks' in her father's drawing-room, hitherto customarily lit only by a fire which 'kept up a lively play of glimmer and shadow in the tall glass over the fireplace' (Oliphant 1998, 27). Wealthier homes gradually installed gas lighting, but by the 1890s, when Oliphant made her last move to Wimbledon, it is probable that the stable, steady glow of the electric light was available. She noted the change that this had made to the coming generation.

> The children of the present day ... find it difficult to understand the terror of the children of an elder age for the dark passages along which so many little heroes and heroines in the old story books made a breathless dart with their hearts in their mouths, not knowing what frightful danger might lurk behind this or that black corner ... There are no dark passages now. One wonders how many people now existing realize what a difference it makes. Ghosts have wholly gone out of fashion with the children, and nobody under the age of fifteen is afraid of them. (Oliphant 1897b, 605)

Her claim is a variation on the usual hypothesis that the rise of the ghost story in the mid-century was a response to the age's scientific materialism. Perhaps the ability of many fictional writers of that period to segue between domestic realism and the supernatural was brought about by the currency of different lighting methods, so that a less technically sophisticated, more superstitious era almost literally lurked in the shadows.

The second reason for the disapproval hinted at in Janet Story's description of her guest's habits may have been Oliphant's working in bed. Such a practice, with its connotations of idleness and late rising, seems to accord particularly ill with the formal elegance that Oliphant presented to the world. In her last decade she wrote from her bed in the early afternoon to her youngest son that late rising had been her besetting sin: 'I only vanquish it now by working in bed as I have always done more or less under one pretence or another' (quoted in Jay 1995, 268). Given the frequent press reports of reading material or bedding catching fire from smouldering candles, one can only marvel at Oliphant's ability to fend off sleep during the night hours. The practice of writing in bed certainly did not improve the legibility of her writing which is notoriously difficult to decipher, partly because her small spidery scrawl made little attempt to discriminate individual letters, let alone to dot i's or cross t's, and the reader is often forced to make out words from their context. I once caused a distinct tremor in the packed manuscript room of the National Library of Scotland by proffering a particularly troublesome passage to a curator who had offered his help.

Not heeding my warning that the word which eluded me could not possibly be what it most appeared to be, he triumphantly supplied his reading *à haute voix*, mistaking an 'e' for a 'u' in the first word of the phrase 'beggary and wretchedness' (Oliphant 2002, 42).

This passage, intended only for the eyes of posthumous readers, had not been copied out by a more legible hand. A series of fair copyists, who freed Oliphant from undertaking this time-consuming activity herself, was one of the secrets behind her extraordinarily prolific career. Ten years passed before her first novel went to print because she had employed her middle brother, an alcoholic (and soon to be disgraced) dissenting minister, to make a copy legible for the printer and to engage in the initial negotiations with publishers. Loyalty prevented her from remarking more than the fact that he had published it 'on his own account,' that is, he had issued it under his own name (as he did four more of her novels, giving himself an authorial pedigree for publishing a further five novels of his own). Other women authors of this period often relied upon male relations to conduct the unseemly process of haggling over terms with publishers. Nor was it uncommon, *in absentia*, to trust close friends and relations with authority to settle copy-editors' queries, as Dickens did with Forster. Oliphant's artist husband was no businessman and Oliphant soon took over dealing with publishers herself.

Evidence about her fair-copying and thus about her revision process is scant, since so few of the manuscripts survive. This may in itself be an indicator that others wrote the fair copies dispatched to publishers that were not retained (manuscripts in another hand have no commercial value, nor the illusion of bringing us nearer to the author's presence). It is clear that when her brother took himself off after their mother's death she missed his services; a year later, in 1855, she lamented, 'I always write with greater comfort when I have the freedom of writing illegibly which is secured by copying my manuscript before dismissing it from my hands – and the chief part of this article was written under the effort of writing a readable hand' (quoted in Jay 1995, 269). It seems plausible that, when her distant cousin, Annie Walker, joined her household in 1866, copying might have been one of the 'secretarial' duties she assumed for her keep. Oliphant left a slip of paper in her autobiographical volumes suggesting that her niece might want to seek Cousin Annie's help '(none so capable)' in editing its pages (Oliphant 2002, 46). Unexpectedly, in 1884, Annie contracted a late marriage to a rich widower, and left Oliphant's household. In 1885, when Oliphant restarted her autobiography, she complained that 'No one belonging to me has energy enough' even to assemble 'the fragments for some one else' to write a biography (Oliphant 2002, 52). It seems reasonable to infer from this remark that she was feeling particularly hard done by in that neither her sons nor her nieces, though all by now in their twenties, unmarried, and dependent on her for their living, had by then assumed Annie's role as the acknowledged resident copyist. Each of them, however, was occasionally pressed into writing letters on her behalf, or revising proofs, which she found 'the one thing intolerable in literature' (quoted in Jay 1995, 272). Although she would scarcely have entrusted these very personal reflections to them while still alive, she had good reason – at a stage when she was so hard pressed that she was mortgaging as yet unwritten novels for the promise of a regular income – to lament what, by her own extraordinarily hard-working standards, she saw as their lassitude.

In the absence of either manuscripts or proofs for the main body of her work, it is particularly difficult to arrive at any sense of how carefully, if at all, she revised individual sentences at the point of composition. If her copious letters are any guide, she rarely made a false step: even long and grammatically complex sentences seemed to unwind themselves onto the page fully formed, although the dash was liberally employed as a way of suggesting the relationship of sub-clauses to the larger whole. The printers, as appears customary in the mid-nineteenth century, were responsible for standardizing her punctuation. One piece of supportive evidence for the fluency of her composition, uninterrupted by heavy excision or revision, comes from her early practice, like Dickens, of estimating final length by the number of pages she had written. She told one disgruntled magazine editor 'my calculation is that two pages of my writing makes about a page of Good Words.' By the 1880s, however, her financial need to assure herself that she was giving good but not excessive measure led her to the practice of counting words 'very much and carefully,' which 'I did not do in the happier days of my youth' (quoted in Jay 1995, 270).

Responding to a reviewer who had attributed her deficiencies to a 'breakneck' speed of composition, she thought herself 'very constant, but very leisurely, in my work ... and my faults must be set down to deficiencies less accidental than want of time. The occasions, now and then, when I am hurried, are those on which I usually do my best' (quoted in Jay 1995, 262). The firm of Blackwoods became so habituated to her using the first proof stage as the opportunity for sometimes extensive revision that they built this leeway into their publishing schedule. She was therefore surprised when the arrival of the 'type printer' at Macmillans in the 1880s, was used, not, as she imagined, to produce this first proof for her to work upon, but as a 'fair copy,' which they then chose to reject (quoted in Jay 1995, 263). When she had the time she would make further revisions between the serial and volume publication of her novels (Oliphant 1998, 521–47). To what extent these were typically determined by the need to produce three volumes of roughly equal length, or volume divisions coincident with plot breaks and climaxes, has yet to be investigated.

What, though, did Oliphant mean by the notion of her writing being 'very constant, but very leisurely'? Having settled her sons as day-boys at Eton, she told John Blackwood in 1867, 'I can work fifteen hours a day at home' (quoted in Jay 1995, 270). Allowing for exaggeration, and her need to explain to him that a trip to Germany meant an alteration to this pace, this still puts her in the league of those who require little sleep. In 1891, abroad again, in Davos, and in mourning for the death of her eldest son, she reviewed her rate of production.

> I have carried it on all this time steadily, a chapter a day, I suppose about twenty pages of an octavo book. Sir Walter [Scott] when he was labouring to pay off his debts, speaks of writing a volume in twelve days I think. I have done it steadily in sixteen. He says no man can keep it up for long – but I have kept it up in spite of everything now for months and months … In addition to this work I wrote a short story (worth thirty pounds) two or three nights after C and D [her remaining son and her niece – both adults] had gone to bed. (Oliphant, 2002, 96)

How did she do it? We should not forget that as her income and her family's needs grew, Oliphant employed more servants, including a cook, and that visits abroad at this stage in her life involved staying in fully catered hotels. Against those nineteenth-century amenities we should set the absence of a literary agent, of the telephone, and of e-mail.

She also enjoyed the variety of her writing life. When she and her mother first targeted *Blackwood's Edinburgh Magazine* it was the premier literary journal of its day, publishing fiction, reviews of contemporary non-fiction, and essays on assorted literary topics. Once habituated to practising these different genres she would grumble when Blackwood 'interdicted her from other work' (Oliphant 1974, 192), as he threatened to do in May 1863, the month before serialization of *The Perpetual Curate* was due to begin. The parcels of new books that regularly arrived for her, whether at home in Windsor, on holiday in St Andrews, or abroad, kept her in the literary swim, and cross-fertilized her own work, prompting her to try her hand at a variety of fictional genres. Moreover, the different personae that she adopted in her fiction and her reviewing, publishing the former under her own name, and the latter in the guise of a male writer, added the extra challenge of writing in character.

Her comparative remoteness from London's literary circles and dinners, and the mutual obligations they built up, lent a certain independence to her opinions. Although she was inclined to bewail her hand-to-mouth freelance existence as the cause of her financial troubles, her sheer reliability as a contributor meant that she was permitted to depart from the Blackwoods' line on particular books and authors. Henry James, a writer thoroughly networked into the social aspects of London's literary life, saw Oliphant's freedom rather differently: 'No woman had ever, for half a century, had her personal "say" so publicly and irresponsibly' (James 1897, 358). It is true that the speed at which Oliphant worked, combined with the distance she would have had to travel to adequate libraries, did not incline her to check facts or quotations. This 'irresponsibility' was by no means exceptional amongst Oliphant's contemporaries (Gaskell displays much the same tendency to quote, or rather misquote, from memory), but to those who prided themselves upon their scholarship it seemed reprehensible. The George Eliot household apparently held up its hands in horror at 'the unprincipledness of even good people like Mrs Oliphant who write of that whereof they know nothing' (Eliot 1954–78, IX, 228).

Her status as an outsider, born and raised in Scotland, transported by her parents to Liverpool for her adolescent years, and living in London only for brief periods, lent her a penetrating eye for the habits and foibles of settled societies, whether the dissenting back streets of Carlingford, the leisured life of England's squirearchy, or the humble life of the Scots manse. Her capacity to address English and Scottish readers made her particularly attractive to Blackwoods as they sought to extend their national reach. Yet the mobility that had taken her from lower middle-class provincial origins to being on tea-taking terms with Queen Victoria also prevented her from achieving an easily identifiable niche in the heritage industry by the time she died. Had she been a kail-yard novelist she might have been more instantly claimed as a Scots possession. The strong financial incentives that work to preserve the creative environment of writers located in places with little other claim on the tourist industry, as was the case with the Brontës and Haworth, or Thomas Hardy and Dorchester, were absent in her case.

The Royal Borough of Windsor already possessed a major attraction, and in any case her fierce pride in her Scots accent made her difficult to fashion into a local genius, despite the fact that she is buried there along with her two sons. Moreover, a year before her death she moved house after thirty years. When she died the century was waning and with it her reputation, in the new age of the aesthete. It was not until the centenary of her death that Windsor honoured her with a blue plaque on the front of what is now a private and much altered dwelling. Fortunately, in spite of her gloomy predictions, her remaining niece summoned the energy to collaborate in assembling the first edition of Oliphant's *Autobiography*, and to pass on personal material to her nephews. The choice of the National Library of Scotland as the chief repository of her papers would surely have pleased her.

So what might we learn from Oliphant's circumstances about the creative process? The list of things to avoid is long. Do not publish, or allow to have published after your death, your misgivings as to the lasting merit of your *oeuvre*, your fears that your kind of writing has had its day. Never accept responsibility for adult relatives, however close, who do not manifest their usefulness to you on a daily basis; their demands will suck you into accepting commissions based on financial need rather than creative enjoyment. Do not give interviews or go on publicity tours, as this merely wastes valuable writing time. If you wish posterity to remember you in your finest writerly hours do not destroy your original manuscripts, and certainly do not dismantle the room, annexe, alcove, or four-poster bed where you achieved your finest triumphs.

If you prefer the positive version of lessons to be derived from Oliphant's creative life, then read her own late story, 'The Library Window,' which tells the tale of a girl, given to 'fantasticating,' and brought up by her culture to believe that only men could enjoy the necessary space, time, and education to write, who nevertheless becomes the compelling narrator of her own life story. To write well you need to be an insatiable reader and be passionate about writing. Test your writing on the nearest available audience; if your family tires of this, then make close friends of your publishers, and entertain them often and well. Oliphant made a point of renting houses within visiting distance of a series of her publishers and threw a legendary party in 1877 on the island of Runnymede to celebrate her connection with the Blackwoods firm (Porter 1898, III, 353). If you find yourself saddled with dispiriting dependants, remember the pleasurable escape from them that imaginative work provides, and, if all else fails, turn them into subject matter. Be flexible, about both where and what you are prepared to write. Try your hand at different genres (Oliphant even ventured the odd poem and drama for domestic performance), and do not despise the art of reviewing or travel writing. But, above all, whatever the personal tragedies that beset you or the publishers' rejections you receive, keep writing, even if you suffer from repetitive strain injury or wear a hole in your right forefinger.

Works Cited

Eliot, George, 1954–78. *The Letters*, ed. G. S. Haight. 9 vols. New Haven: Yale University Press.

Gaskell, E. C., 1997. *The Life of Charlotte Brontë*, ed. E. Jay. Harmondsworth: Penguin.

James, H., 1914. *London Notes* (August 1897), reprinted in *Notes for Novelists*. London: J. M. Dent.

Jay, E., 1995. *Mrs Oliphant: 'A Fiction to herself': A Literary Life*. Oxford: Clarendon Press.

Oliphant, M. O. W., 1856. *Christian Melville*. London: David Bogue.

Oliphant, M. O. W., 1897a. *Annals of a Publishing House: William Blackwood and His Sons: Their Magazine and Friends*. 2 vols. Edinburgh: William Blackwood & Sons.

Oliphant, M. O. W., 1897b. ''Tis Sixty years Since,' *Blackwoods Edinburgh Magazine*, 161 (May 1897): 599–624.

Oliphant, M. O. W., 1974. *The Autobiography and Letters of Mrs Margaret Oliphant*, ed. Mrs Harry Coghill, reprint and intro. Q. D. Leavis. Leicester: Leicester University Press.

Oliphant, M. O. W., 1998. *Miss Marjoribanks*, ed. Elisabeth Jay. Harmondsworth: Penguin.

Oliphant, M. O. W., 2002. *The Autobiography of Margaret Oliphant*, ed. Elisabeth Jay. Peterborough, ON: Broadview Press.

Porter, Mrs Gerald, 1898. *Annals of a Publishing House: John Blackwood*. 3 vols. Edinburgh: William Blackwood & Sons.

Ritchie, A. T., 1913. *From the Porch*. London: Smith, Elder.

Story, J. L., 1913. *Later Reminiscences*. Glasgow: James Maclehose & Sons.

Sturgis, H. O., 1899. 'A Sketch from Memory,' *Temple Bar*, 118 (Oct. 1899): 233–48.

Literary Archives: the British Library

GRAEME HARPER interviews JAMIE ANDREWS

GH: What does your job involve?

JA: I'm Head of Modern Literary Manuscripts. 'Modern,' from the days when the British Museum contained the Library, was post-medieval. In theory, my section is 1600 onwards. In practice, a lot of the work we do is with contemporary twentieth-century material. 'Literary' is defined in its widest sense, not just the archives and manuscripts of writers, whether they're novelists, poets, playwrights, but anyone significant in production or reception. We have archives of critics, publishers, agents, and so on.

'Manuscripts' used to be fairly easy to define, but now we're at a cusp where there are still traditional manuscripts, which are handwritten or typewritten or word processed – still physical objects. But now there are also e-manuscripts, which could be emails, could be Word documents, could be data sets, could be Excel files, could be any digital text. The only way we can describe manuscripts now is as unique items. They could be letters or emails. They could be printed *non*-unique items, which were collected by the creators. Press clippings, for example, will exist elsewhere in the Library in, say, the newspaper section, but they reclaim uniqueness in being selected and pasted in by the particular creator of the archive. We're not really set up to curate, preserve or interpret objects, but now and again there are even certain objects that are so closely entwined with the meaning of a collection as a whole that we will take them in.

GH: What about acquisition and making them available?

JA: When we take in new materials, whether by purchase or donation, we process them so that they can be interpreted in a meaningful form. With archives, cataloguing is very important, though it doesn't always get a high profile. Say we take in fifty boxes. We have to sort them if they've come in unsorted, arrange them, and identify preservation needs before anyone can use them, internally or externally. Getting them out there, after clearing copyright issues, takes a variety of forms depending on the audience we want. There may be a way to make new collections available externally by the Web. It may be just encouraging people to come and study them in the reading room. And it may be exhibiting them, either online or in the galleries. It might be writing or delivering papers. It's trying to get the collections out to a wide variety of audiences in different ways.

GH: How is the decision made on what to collect, and who makes it?

JA: The kind of stuff we deal with has economic value and that is decided on the basis of comparators. With unique material it's not that easy to find those comparators. How do you compare a Beckett letter with a Pinter letter? However, what we're really concerned with is research value. We hope the budget will be there to purchase what we think is valuable for research. There are two aspects to this. On the one hand, every research library's collection development policy looks backwards to fill gaps, adding to material that already exists where we've become a research base for Ted Hughes or whoever. So it's defined by previous collecting. On the other hand, it also looks forward, to identify new trends, new writers we think will be important. Clearly, in this aspect, some subjective knowledge and personal taste will come into it, though it is backed up by assessments of the research background in the UK and America, in terms of what's been taught in undergraduate and postgraduate study.

When the question of modern literary manuscripts comes up, there's always the sense that American institutions have been hoovering up this kind of material. One reason is that they started much earlier than us. They started collecting contemporary British writers at the beginning of the twentieth century, partly because their teaching used more modern authors than British universities. They needed this kind of material to support it. Teaching has a very real impact, especially in America, since the main collections there are not the national institutions but university research libraries.

The third way in which value is decided – the only criteria that are actually written down and operate at a national level – are where we have to decide whether an archive is of sufficient value that it should be accepted by the nation for the national collections. It doesn't matter where it goes at this stage; the question will be whether it should be accepted by the nation to offset inheritance tax or various other tax liabilities after the death of the writer. In that case, you do break down the definition of value in two ways: the pre-eminence of the writer and whether a particular object is so closely entwined with the history of the country that it would be unimaginable for it to leave the shores. That works for both export licences and for acceptance in lieu.

GH: How much of the material you mention is not literary manuscripts or draft materials. How much is letters, scribbles, doodles …?

JA: Almost everything that is unique is considered. Whenever this comes up in popular press it gets taken to absurd lengths – Zadie Smith's shopping list or whatever. Nevertheless, when we look at archives we're looking at how each piece relates to the others. Each is not an individual item in the way that printed books are a succession of individual items. An archive is an undivided whole in which every item adds value to the others, from the pristine quality drafts to the odd scrap of paper.

GH: Has it always been seen this way?

JA: When British institutions first decided to deal with living writers, in the late 1950s (to a great degree at the instigation of people like Philip Larkin, both a poet and a librarian), the definition of what manuscripts were was very narrow. When they first set up the National Manuscript Collection of Contemporary Poets, first they only looked at poets – who were deemed to be the most suited to manuscript study – and then they only looked at their poetic notebooks or drafts. So correspondence, for example, was excluded from the collection. For example, the Library (the Museum at the time) took in the poetic notebooks of Kathleen Raine, but not her autobiographical material as it was in prose, even though written by a poet. Keith Douglas's poetry couldn't be put next to his prose pieces, like *Alamein to Zem Zem*. There was also a sense that the collection should only be representative. There are crazy reports from the mid-1960s, I think, saying that Auden and Hughes and Larkin were now adequately represented, because one poetical notebook of each was held.

From the 1970s, though, the Library opened up to all creative writing. Initially, they were reluctant to collect playwrights' works, perhaps because of the difficulty of actually tying down the archive of an ephemeral performance, but that passed. They also widened collection to correspondence and other materials.

Note that the creator of the archive isn't us, it's the novelist or dramatist or poet who retains or destroys material at will. It's interesting to see that some people keep absolutely every item of fan mail, circulars even, while others whittle it down to a succession of star names. The selection process is part of the archive.

GH: Yet the British Library is as much a creator of literary heritage as it is its holder, in the way things get collected and displayed, or people promote certain parts of the archive. Is that a manipulation of the creative environment itself?

JA: We want to make all our material equally available to whoever needs it [the British Library welcomes teachers as much as researchers as readers; both must demonstrate a need to use the collection]. That's where cataloguing is the most un-intrusive form of work that we do: we haven't influenced what's there, we just take it in, describe it, and make it available to whoever logs on to the catalogue. If something's not catalogued it's invisible, and only available to those in the know who may, for whatever reason, have picked up that we've acquired this collection. Over the last couple of years we've developed a cataloguing backlog strategy, so that within three years pretty much everything will be catalogued. The catalogues are available online, externally, so anyone can have access via the variety of ways of searching.

On the other hand, we do pick out certain things for exhibitions, online resources, and so on; we should – and do – interpret our material, consciously and openly. But also, very recently, we're starting to consider ourselves a forum for further creativity. We've had all sorts of plays or novels that have been put on or written as a result of contact with our primary resources and original materials. It's just making people aware of what's here; the creative industries, the performing industries, have access to all this and can use it to stimulate their own work.

For instance, we've got the collection of the plays submitted to the Lord Chamberlain for censorship: every play that was ever publicly performed in Britain between 1737 and 1968. An unimaginable number of plays, most of which weren't published – obviously, only a tiny percentage of plays performed are ever published – and most of them not known at all. There have been various small fringe theatres coming in and looking back at these neglected plays. They've been picking things out that are of interest, either for dramatic or social quality, and putting them on. Take the Pinter production on last year [2007] at the National Theatre. *The Hothouse* was written in 1958, but published decades later. The director [Ian Rickson] came in to look at the archive, compared the original draft of 1958 with the later published version, and amalgamated them, with Pinter's permission.

GH: Take your large exhibition recently, *The European Avant Garde 1900–1937*, with a Joyce manuscript, recordings of poets and commentators in continental languages, Schoenberg's Five Orchestral Pieces, David Gascoigne's 1930s notebooks, and more. How does the process of mounting an exhibition work? Do you start with a theme, with a set of potential representative writers, with personal tastes, with …?

JA: We're constrained by the availability of space. We can fit several hundred items in the large gallery, but that's several hundred out of the 150 million items we hold. There's also a smaller space in the front hall where you can fit about a hundred items. There are also time constraints. In the large space you can have two exhibitions a year. In the smaller space you can have three exhibitions a year. After that it's a mixture. There are the anniversaries that we look forward to. In 2016 we'll do something fairly large about Shakespeare, for example.

Then there are other opportunities: *Avant Garde*, for instance, tied in with the opening of Eurostar at St Pancras. The next small-scale one in the front hall gallery, which I'm doing, is on post-war theatre [September 2008]. It's both forty years since censorship in theatre ended, and the end of a five-year project we've been doing with Sheffield University, to investigate post-war theatre through oral history interviews. In terms of pre-eminent archives, we've been acquiring Olivier, Pinter, and so on, but also balancing that with the individual ground-eye view of that period of theatre. We've done oral history interviews with anyone involved with British theatre between 1945 and 1968: stage hands, people who sold ice-creams and tickets, audience members … not just London performances but also rep. in the north of England and across the country. That's been absolutely fascinating. For the first time we're going to be exhibiting the archives and interviews side by side. The exhibition in September will have an iconic manuscript, let's say Osborne's handwritten draft of *The Entertainer*, next to an audio recording of a stagehand who worked on the lighting rig at the Royal Court when it was being performed, next to a picture of Olivier acting in that production.

Finally, there are ideas from outside the Library, from academics, writers, and institutions, and internal suggestions by Library staff. The Curatorial Interpretation Group considers them all, and considers questions of funding.

GH: Going back to the North American context, and the big libraries there. Are there any obvious cultural differences in the use and display of literary archives?

JA: The stakeholders are different. There, a lot of the key collecting institutions are linked with university research libraries. These don't receive much public funding so rely on endowments – for example, those from alumni. Thus, they're not working towards public targets, and so they're not always as concerned with access in the ways that we are.

Moreover, North American libraries make a great effort to attract readers and users from across the student body, not just from the humanities. They want to attract people doing law and medicine, people who go on to become rich lawyers and doctors, who may have been enthused by the literary manuscripts and recognize that in their giving. The libraries are very open about it. So they're keyed into a different demographic, and that feeds into the sense that they provide a niche service for top-class researchers. They don't necessarily always stretch their access across such a broad range of audiences.

On the other hand, at the moment 80 per cent of our funding is from the government, and only 20 per cent from our own sources (giving, shop sales, and so on). So there has to be a sense that, while our primary audiences are researchers and academics, we want to satisfy a broad range of audiences since they're all contributing to it essentially: PhD students down to local primary schools, and everything in between. Exhibitions are for general interest. An audience who hits the exhibition can be someone who was intending to be in the reading room and got waylaid, or someone who comes directly to see the exhibition and won't be looking at the items in reading rooms. So I think the crucial cultural difference between the UK and US libraries is in the range of users.

GH: How many times do ethical questions come up over literary archives, in relation to such things as writers' private correspondence?

JA: When I was saying we had a duty to make things available, it's not necessarily making all things available to anyone in a reading room. There's different ways of making it available. A general-interest user wouldn't necessarily need to flick through, say, William Blake's notebook. In fact, very few people can or should because of the fragility, which is why it's been fully digitized, so you can turn the pages virtually.

In terms of personal information, we work within the current legal framework. The Data Protection Act limits access to personal information, defined across a range of categories (sexuality, health, finance, *et cetera*). That protects living people. As soon as you're dead you don't benefit from data protection in the same way as those alive do. So this information can suddenly come into the public domain, if someone dies. But as long as people are living – and in dealing with contemporary manuscripts we think this is really important – their information is protected. When we catalogue material the cataloguers are trained to look for personal information, and where they feel it would come under data protection then they restrict it for the lifetime of the person. There's just a short entry in the catalogue saying that the documents are restricted under the recent Data Protection Act. Before the legislation, such decisions were made by individuals. We're a public institution, and under freedom of information people have a right to access our information, but when it comes to living people data protection trumps freedom of information.

In terms of copyright, again we work within the law. Often when we purchase items or receive them as a donation we get the actual physical documents, but not the intellectual property rights. Hence, we have to be aware of copyright just like anyone else when we want to digitize them or mount them or quote extensively from them. Other times, we also acquire the copyright. This frees up the kinds of things we can do with the material, but it also means someone here has to administrate that copyright when other people want to use it.

There's a difference between copyright for published and unpublished material. In theory, up until recently, copyright for unpublished material was perpetual. That could run to absurd lengths, so an unpublished Shakespeare manuscript, for instance, (not that any exist), would be in copyright. In practice, copyright on manuscript hadn't really been upheld much beyond the last two hundred years or so, so you used to be on fairly safe ground for anything before that. That's now changed; from 1988 the seventy years *post-mortem auctoris* (the rule for published works) also applies to unpublished works. A period of adjustment was allowed, so the law won't kick in until 2039. But on 1 January 2040 all sorts of unpublished material that has previously been in copyright will suddenly come out of copyright. There's going to be a stampede by publishers, researchers, and public institutions to make the material more widely available than we're currently able to do.

GH: People now can access so much original creative material via the

Web. The size of the potential audience has increased, but have potential violations of copyright, challenges to creative ownership, also gone up?

JA: Different groups of writers respond differently to that. I know some poets are particularly worried by this because, of course, a poem can be very easily transcribed, whacked on the Web, maybe a hundred lines long. It's a lot more of an investment of time and effort to put a whole novel online. When we put anything on our own website we minutely observe all copyright restrictions. But there's nothing to stop someone coming to a reading room and transcribing by hand the entirety of a manuscript. Although we make it clear that what they do with it afterwards has to be in accordance with the copyright law, we can't actually follow this up. So perhaps copyright law should be relaxed in recognition of this new environment – I know that's very controversial!

GH: How much of the desire to see the original object is about a fascination with literary culture, a fascination with writers' lives?

JA: Compared to works of art, the kind of money that we're talking about to acquire a literary archive is small fry. In the most recent survey in 2006 the average price for an archive was £50,000, and would rarely exceed a million. In fact, there were only two occasions since 2000 where it did – one was Harold Pinter. So there isn't that kind of fascination with how much they cost, like paintings bought for £20 million. Instead, it's a fascination with how great works that people may have studied since an early age get written. People don't realize this writing went through a laborious process of drafting and redrafting and cancellation and starting again – all this hesitation and deviation that went into the final work with which they're so familiar.

GH: Do you think 'I'm dealing with heritage here'?

JA: Probably to a larger degree than you might expect, because we're not just preserving the works of the greatest writers in Britain, we're preserving a picture of Britain's literary heritage – which can include writers, agents, publishers. … If you look at the kind of funding bodies that we might go to – a Heritage Lottery Fund, the National Heritage Memorial Fund – these bodies are not concerned necessarily with literary pre-eminence but with an overall view of our heritage.

GH: And your big dream?

JA: What would be great is the unexpected find. A notebook of William Blake turned up just fifty years ago. It wasn't known about before: drafts, handwritten drafts of 'Tiger,' 'London,' and so on. It's something like that that I'd like. There are no real manuscripts of Shakespeare. There are a couple of documents which may or may not be in his hand, some of which are legal documents, and which aren't strictly speaking literary manuscripts. So I guess I'd have to say that if Shakespeare's archive turned up I'd be quite happy …

Glue and Daydreams: Trollope at Work

N. JOHN HALL

ANYONE WHO KNOWS ANYTHING about Trollope knows that he got up very early every morning and wrote thousands of words. Those claiming a bit more knowledge gleefully describe how he would finish one novel and then invariably begin another the very next day. Some, in a further refinement, claim that if he finished a novel halfway through his pre-dawn writing stint, he would immediately start on the next one. These embellishments are inaccurate, but the unvarnished reality, unambiguously enshrined in the archival record, is nonetheless amazing.

Anthony Trollope (1815–82) produced some seventy books, among which were forty-seven novels (compare this with fifteen for Dickens, eight for Thackeray, seven for George Eliot, four for Charlotte Brontë); five volumes of short stories, a handful of uncollected short stories; four large travel books and a slight one on Iceland; books on Caesar, Thackeray, Palmerston, and Cicero; four collections of 'Sketches' (hunting types, clergymen, travellers, and tradesmen); an unpublished book of social criticism; an autobiography; and enough essays and reviews to fill two or three more volumes. Yet he produced most of these while serving as an energetic and highly placed officer of the Post Office, during which years he considered his postal work his principal occupation. Indeed, Henry James thought that Trollope's experiences in the Post Office might account for his fondness for transcribing letters in his fiction: 'No contemporary story-teller deals so much in letters ... the modern English epistle ... is his unfailing resource' (Smalley 1969, 539).

1834–1841

Naturally, over his long career, Trollope's writing habits were not constant. Nor were his postal working environments anything like constant during his many years in the Post Office. He got off to a slow start in both careers. In 1834, when Trollope began to work for the Post Office, he was nineteen. His childhood and youth, as recounted in An Autobiography, had been deeply unhappy, chiefly as a result of

his impoverished standing at Winchester and Harrow, schools of the
well-to-do. After his father's long and disastrous efforts to become a
gentleman farmer at Harrow, affairs came to such a pass that the family
had to flee to the Continent and Bruges. From there, Trollope's mother
used her London connections to secure him a junior clerkship in the
office of the Secretary (the chief officer) of the Post Office, housed in
the General Post Office Headquarters in St Martin's-le-Grand. The pay
was £90 per annum, the hours ten to four. Trollope's duties consisted
chiefly in copying letters into a letter book and minutes into a minute
book. Such work, boring and unchallenging, frustrated the energetic
young man, and he came perilously close to being dismissed for tardi-
ness and sloppy work. He was also always in financial troubles. And he
moved in self-described fast company; there is the familiar story of the
woman bursting into the clerks' room and demanding to know when
he would marry her daughter.

In 1876 Trollope wrote:

> I hated the office, I hated my work. More than all I had hated my
> idleness. I had often told myself since I left school that the only
> career in life within my reach was that of an author, and the only
> mode of authorship open to me that of a writer of novels. In a
> journal which I read and destroyed a few years since, I found the
> matter argued out before I had been in the Post Office two years.
> Parliament was out of the question. I had not means to go to the Bar.
> In official life, such as that to which I had been introduced, there
> did not seem to be any opening for real success. Pens and paper I
> could command. Poetry I did not believe to be within my grasp. The
> drama, too, which I would fain have chosen, I believed to be above
> me. For history, biography, or essay writing I had not sufficient erudi-
> tion. But I thought it possible that I might write a novel.
>
> (Trollope 1950, 52–3)

However, the only writing he did at this time seems to have been
the journal (later destroyed), which covered roughly the decade of the
1830s, and a desultory commonplace book for the years 1835–40. The
latter has but twenty-two entries, many of them brief references to
Italian and Spanish writers of the past: Alfieri, Boccaccio, Cervantes,
Calderon. He had not read these authors, only read about them in
either J. C. L. Sismonde de Sismondi or A. W. von Schlegel's works.
But the one non-literary entry should interest us here. Under 'Order –
method' he writes: 'I am myself in all the pursuits (God help them) &

practices of my life most disorderly & unmethodical.' This failing has brought him near to 'utter ruin.' He shifts some of the blame to his parents: 'The first impression which a parent should fix on the mind of a child, is I think love of order. It is the reins by which all virtues are kept in their proper place – & the vices, with whom the virtues run in one team, are controlled.' Order is 'vital' in religion, studies, accounts, diet, and cleanliness. In regard to accounts, he elaborates: 'A man entering life wd make no bad bargain in dividing half his last shilling to buying a red book with blue perpendicular lines. Those blue lines so hated by the young gentry of small fortunes, would fill themselves with figures on the right sheet, were they properly attended to in every monetary transaction' (Trollope 1983, II, 1027–8). This accords perfectly with the practice of Trollope the mature writer, evidenced so spectacularly later on in the 'working diaries' for his novels.

1841–1851

In 1841 Trollope managed to get himself transferred to the Central District of Ireland as assistant or 'clerk' to the superintendent or 'Surveyor.' His headquarters were Banagher, Kings County (today County Offaly), where his new boss, one James Drought, a cantankerous and lazy official, deputed most of his work to his ambitious assistant. Trollope, who had chafed at the day-long sedentary work of a London clerk, took immediately to travelling about the country by horseback. He was a man of far above average physical strength and seemingly indefatigable energies, and he found himself at last. During his very first three weeks on the job he spent sixteen days away from home, and travelled 316 miles visiting a dozen different towns. His job was to inspect post offices, check their books, seek out irregularities, and investigate complaints. After some time he was given the additional task of expanding the rural posts, seeing to it that the mail arrived at isolated villages and homes. He loved the work.

His salary rose to £180 but was supplemented by travelling expenses. In order to recoup the latter funds, he had to keep a scrupulous 'travel diary' indicating his daily whereabouts, miles travelled, and expenses for bed and board. In this travel diary he was doing precisely the kind of orderly record-keeping that, in his earlier Commonplace Book, he had accused himself of not practising. In his very first year in Ireland, his income, including travel allowances, rose by his own account to exactly

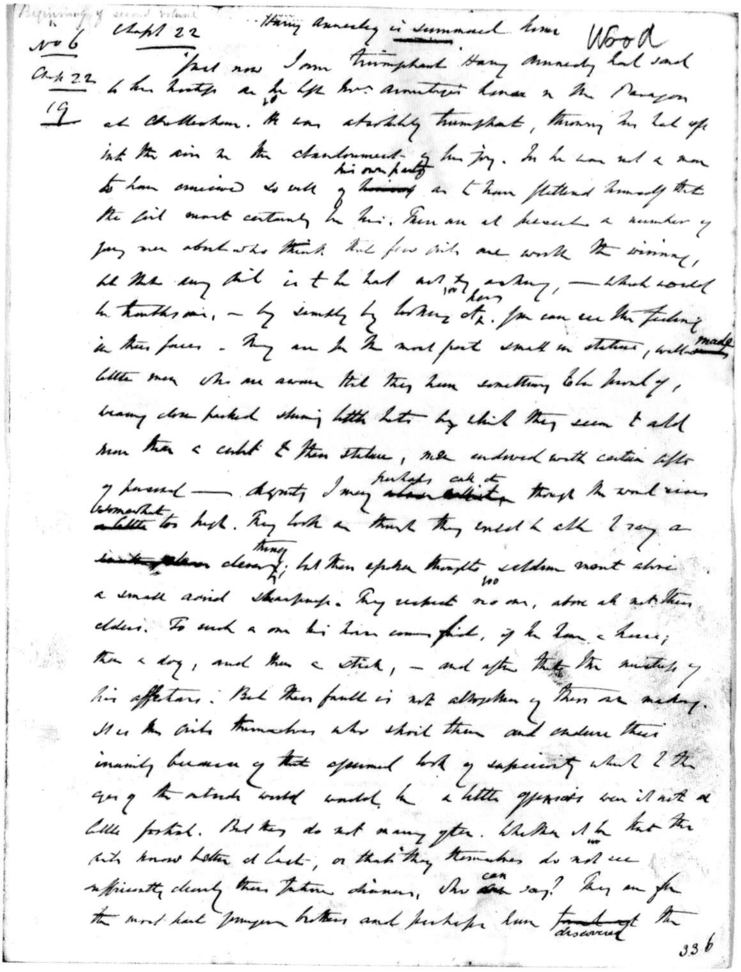

Plate 2: Manuscript page from *Mr. Scarborough's Family* (the beginning of Chapter 22, page 19 of instalment number six, written in June 1881). The name Wood at the top is the compositor's. Like almost all of Trollope's manuscript pages, it contains only minor revisions.

£313.4s.2d.[1] Moreover, in rural Ireland the cost of living was drastically less than in London. He was never again in financial difficulty.

His writing career, however, got off to a sluggish start. He began his first novel, *The Macdermots of Ballycloran*, in 1843, worked on it for two years, and saw it published in 1847, when he was thirty-two. Between 1846 and 1847, he wrote his second novel, *The Kellys and The O'Kellys*; and between 1848 and 1849 (exact dates are lacking) he completed his third novel, *La Vendée* (thought by many his least successful fiction). None of these books sold.

There is no evidence of how, in these years, he worked his novel writing into a busy Post Office schedule, nor of whether he wrote various drafts or did much revision. Trollope's earliest extant manuscript (that of his fifth book, the non-fiction *New Zealander*, which was not published in his lifetime) dates from 1855 to 1856; the earliest manuscript for a novel to survive, *Framley Parsonage*, dates from 1859 to 1860. However, it seems unlikely that, even from the beginning, Trollope ever did much revision. Later on his written words streamed onto the paper as though dictated to a secretary: a friend recorded that Trollope used as a 'favourite expression' the words 'told himself' to describe his novel writing (Bradley 1882, 70). The many manuscripts that survive are as first written out and dispatched to the printers. They are not second drafts or fair copies, but the original first pages, uncannily clean for the most part of any but the occasional small change – one word substituted for another, occasionally a phrase substituted for another.[2] The manuscript page reprinted here (Plate 2), taken from a late novel, *Mr. Scarborough's Family*, is typical. Trollope claimed that keeping a journal (the one he destroyed) 'had habituated me to the rapid use of pen and ink, and taught me how to express myself with facility' (Trollope 1950, 42). Another help was writing Post Office reports of which he produced 'thousands' and over which he took pains to compose immediately into final form. He seems to have regarded making a revised version of anything – novel, report, or letter – as somehow dishonest, or at least unhelpful. Rewriting, 'polishing,' as he

1   Trollope's six travel diaries survive in the Parrish Collection, Princeton University Library; through them one can determine Trollope's exact whereabouts on almost every day from 1841 until his retirement from the Post Office twenty-six years later.
2   In 1878 at the bidding of an editor, Trollope, in a most unusual move, reduced the 'four-volume' *Duke's Children* manuscript to the more customary three-volume length. Stephen Amarnick is preparing for publication an uncut edition of the novel.

called it, led in him to 'the smell of the polishing oil,' or, in another
favourite metaphor, made the rewritten work appear to be 'upon stilts'
(Trollope 1950, 135). He also thought rewriting a waste of time. But
during the early Irish years the facility and discipline that would amaze
the world was still far off.

1851–1859

In 1851, Rowland Hill, Secretary of the Post Office, 'lent' Trollope to
the South West District of England because of his exceptional energy
and efficiency in extending the rural posts in Ireland. His new task
involved laying out the routes for rural letter carriers – he 'did' Devon,
Cornwall, Somerset, and much of Dorset, the Channel Islands (where
he introduced the first pillar boxes), parts of Oxfordshire, Wiltshire,
Gloucestershire, Worcestershire, Herefordshire, Monmouthshire, and
the six counties of southern Wales. He moved about continually on
horseback, and counted his three years in so doing as the happiest of
his life, even if his part-time writing career was suspended. Then, one
Saturday evening, in Salisbury, 'whilst wandering there on a midsummer
evening round the purlieus of the cathedral I conceived the story of *The
Warden*' (Trollope 1950, 92). This was on 22 May 1852 (according to
his travel diary). He didn't write anything down, but 'thought about'
the novel till the following June, when he wrote the first chapter.
Just at this time he was recalled to Ireland to be Acting Surveyor of
the Northern District, and only in October of the following year was
he able to mail the manuscript of this short (one-volume) novel to
publisher William Longman. On that very day Trollope was named
Surveyor of the Northern District of Ireland, twenty years after starting
as a clerk in St Martin's-le-Grand. Longman, the oldest and most pres-
tigious London publishing house, accepted the book and brought out it
quickly, in January 1855. *The Warden* had very real critical success, and
Trollope commented that although 'The novel-reading world did not
go mad about *The Warden* … I soon felt it had not failed as the others
had failed … and I could discover that people around me knew that I
had written a novel' (Trollope 1950, 98).

But six weeks later, Longman sent him a discouraging account of
the sales of *The Warden*. Thereupon Trollope broke off writing the
sequel, *Barchester Towers* (by then up to eighty-five manuscript pages),
and instead worked on a book of non-fiction, essays about honesty in
British life (misleadingly called *The New Zealander*). Longman turned

this book down flat. It took a year and a half before Trollope returned, on 12 May 1856, to fiction and to *Barchester Towers*.

Determined now to work more industriously and more systematically at his writing, he adopted two strategies. The first was to write while travelling. In his postal work, the railway had by now largely replaced horseback and horse-drawn carriages. Trollope recalled, 'Like others [during train travel], I used to read – though Carlyle has since told me that a man when travelling should not read, but "sit still and label his thoughts." But if I intended to make a profitable business out of my writing, and, at the same time, to do my best for the Post Office, I must turn these hours to more account than I could even by reading.' Trollope made up a 'writing tablet,' and soon found that he could 'write as quickly in a railway-carriage as I could at my desk' (Trollope 1950, 103). He finished *Barchester Towers* on 9 November of that year, the greater part of the book having been written in railway carriages. Years later he would have carpenters build writing desks in his cabins on ocean-crossing steamers.

The second system adopted at this time was a 'working diary' for each novel. He was forty-one, and, as if prompted by that Commonplace Book of the 1830s, he adapted ledger-like, columned record-keeping to his writing: marking off the days in weekly sections, entering daily the number of pages written each session, then noting the week's total. His 'page' – always the same size – held approximately 250 words. He set a goal of forty manuscript pages per week. He would have preferred to work seven days, but of course there were weeks when he could manage only a few days, and some weeks when illness or pressures of postal work kept him from writing altogether. Yet he generally managed the forty pages per week; on a few occasions he pushed himself to more than a hundred pages in a week. The working diaries were an extraordinary exercise in self-discipline. For whereas his postal work had its daily and weekly obligations – including frequent and lengthy written reports – his earlier novel writing had been under no compulsion other than his own will, and the upshot had been what Trollope called 'spasmodic' results. Now, he wanted a self-induced system of 'task work.' Henceforth, Trollope wrote under the watchfulness, as it were, of these diaries, with the result that 'if at any time I have slipped into idleness for a day or two, the record of that idleness has been there, staring me in the face, and demanding of me increased labour, so that the deficiency might be supplied.' A week without a sufficient number of pages was 'a blister on my eye,' and a month would have been 'a sorrow to my heart' (Trollope 1950, 119). Lapses were indicated by entries such as

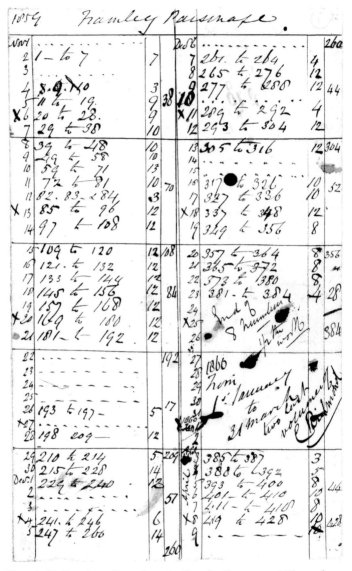

Plate 3: Trollope's working diary for *Framley Parsonage*, 1 November 1859 to 9 April 1860. It records the date (with 'X' to indicate Sunday) and the number of pages written each day, and gives daily, weekly and cumulative page totals. It also shows that he broke off between 1 January 1860 and 31 March 1860 to write the 'two last volumes of C. Richmond', and resumed *Framley Parsonage* on 3 April.

'Sore throat,' 'Ill,' 'Hunting,' 'Alas,' or 'Ah me!' But such interruptions were to remain relatively few; by and large the working diaries record a steady outpouring of pages that must have provided a deep source of satisfaction. The intervals between the writing of his novels would vary greatly, ranging from three months down to the three instances when Trollope completed a novel and began a new one the next day (never did he begin a new novel the very day he finished one). A rough average, for what it is worth, was about six weeks between novels.[3] The diary-regulated writing would lead to startling results: with *Barchester Towers*, written at a pace five times faster than that which generated *The Warden*, Trollope's famous, or infamous, productivity took hold, and for good. [Plate 3]

During the remainder of the 1850s, Trollope wrote *The Three Clerks*, *Doctor Thorne*, and *The Bertrams*, a travel book on the West Indies (where Trollope had been sent on a postal mission; his travel books, for which he did not usually keep a diary, were for the most part composed during the travels), a handful of short stories, and began an Irish novel, *Castle Richmond*. Various reviewers were objecting that he was writing too much, but Trollope ignored these complaints. Years later in *An Autobiography* he said, with some irony, that after finishing *Doctor Thorne* he determined to excel 'if not in quality, at any rate in quantity.' 'My novels,' he continued, 'whether good or bad, have been as good as I could make them. Had I taken three months of idleness between each they would have been no better' (Trollope 1950, 122).

1860–1867

Difficult as it is to believe, Trollope by the end of 1859 had not yet quite hit his full writing stride. Although his Post Office career, and, as of late, his writing career as well, had been eminently successful, he hankered for a return to England and to London. When the Surveyorship for the Eastern District of England opened up Secretary Rowland Hill had no practical choice other than to grant Trollope's request for the transfer, though there was no love lost between them. Accordingly Trollope was able to move his wife and sons into a large house at Waltham Cross

---

[3] Trollope's working diaries are in the Michael Sadleir Collection in the Bodleian Library, Oxford. If someone wished to determine the exact date on which Trollope wrote out Mrs Proudie's heart attack or Lizzie Eustace's stealing her own diamonds, he or she could, with some little assiduity, readily do so.

in Hertfordshire, some twelve miles north of London. Operating from his home, he would henceforth criss-cross his large district continually: Essex, Suffolk, Norfolk, Cambridgeshire, Hungtingdonshire, and the eastern parts of Hertfordshire and Bedfordshire.

The official transfer was to be effective in January 1860, but before that happened Trollope made a move that would have repercussions for the remainder of his writing career. He wrote to Thackeray, editor of an about-to-be-commenced magazine, *The Cornhill*, and offered some short stories. Instead, and to Trollope's delight, Thackeray and the magazine's publisher, George Smith, asked him to produce a major (three-volume) novel for the launch of the magazine – the story to be serialized in sixteen monthly instalments. For this Trollope was offered £1000, almost twice his most recent promised payment for *Castle Richmond*, the Irish novel he was writing for Chapman & Hall. He hurried to London, where Edward Chapman graciously said he might take *Castle Richmond* to *The Cornhill*. Trollope then went to see George Smith, who said he didn't want an Irish novel, he wanted 'an English tale, on English life, with a clerical flavour' – a Barsetshire novel (Trollope 1950, 142). Trollope wrote that the money offered was so good that 'had a couple of archbishops been demanded, I should have produced them' (Trollope 1879, 51).

Trollope, in the railway carriage back to Dublin, completed the first pages of *Framley Parsonage*, the English tale with a clerical flavour. The first page of the working diary for the novel, reproduced here, shows his almost superhuman ability to write quickly and to order. The agreement with Smith called for delivery of the first instalment or 'number' of the novel on 1 December. He had, in fact, by 8 November (one week into writing) completed this much, forty-eight manuscript pages (twenty-four *Cornhill* pages); by 23 December he had completed eight numbers or one half of the novel, whereupon he broke off and wrote, from 1 January through to 31 March 1860, the last two volumes of *Castle Richmond* for Chapman & Hall. In April he resumed *Framley Parsonage*. As for writing two novels – so to say – at one time, Trollope commented in his *Autobiography* that doing so presented no problem to him: 'Many of us live in different circles; and when we go from our friends in town to our friends in the country, we do not usually fail to remember the little details of the one life or the other ... In our lives we are always weaving novels, and we manage to keep the different tales distinct' (Trollope 1950, 156).

In the midst of removing from Ireland and setting up a new establishment in England, Trollope added yet another facet to his *modus operandi.* It may indeed have begun in Ireland, but Trollope in *An Auto-biography* places it here. He records that he brought with him from Ireland his Irish groom, Barney, who was instructed to call Trollope at 5.00 am every morning so that he could be at his desk by 5.30. For this service, which included bringing a cup of coffee, Barney was paid an additional £5 yearly. Trollope wrote that in all the years at Waltham Cross Barney was never late: 'I do not know that I ought not to feel that I owe more to him than to any one else for the success I have had. By beginning at that hour I could complete my literary work before I dressed for breakfast' (Trollope 1950, 271). The first half-hour was spent rereading the previous day's work, and then, with his watch open before him, he strove to write a page, or 250 words, every fifteen minutes, or some ten pages daily, 1000 words an hour, or 2500 words a day. One story goes that George Eliot 'positively quivered' when Trollope explained his method to her, and she told him that there were days when she could not write a line. Trollope gallantly offered that with 'imaginative work like yours that is quite natural; but with my mechanical stuff it's a sheer matter of industry. It's not the head that does it – it's cobbler's wax on the seat and sticking to my chair!' He is said to have pointed to this seat of inspiration with an 'inelegant vigour of gesture that sent a thrill of horror through the polite circle there assembled' (Harrison 1895, 185–6; Morley and Ward 1883, 49).[4] The cobbler's glue metaphor was commonplace with him, turning up in his letters and in *An Autobiography*.

Trollope's daily production over the years was under ten pages per sitting, nor was it anywhere near consistent, often varying between as few as four and as many as sixteen pages. The fastest burst of his writing career came in June 1864, when for fourteen days straight he composed fifteen pages of *Miss Mackenzie*; his most productive single day seems to have been 16 June 1867 when he wrote twenty pages of *Linda Tressel* (he regularly managed more pages per day when writing short novels). Interruptions kept his production down (if that is the way to put it): illness, holidays, extra postal work, unusually difficult travel, and most especially, other writing tasks, such as travel books, articles, reviews, and short stories. Naturally, a short novel, and one written during a holiday, had a better chance of being written uninterruptedly. *Lady*

---

[4]   On the other hand, George Eliot said 'I am not at all sure that, but for Anthony Trollope, I should ever have planned my studies on so extensive a scale for *Middlemarch*, or that I should, through all of its episodes, have perse-vered with it to the close' (Escott 1913, 184–5).

Anna (written in 1871 entirely aboard ship while going to visit his son in Australia) had but one day of stoppage, for illness; *Dr. Wortle's School* (written in April 1879 on holiday at a rural rectory in Northampton-shire lent him by a friend, and composed in exactly twelve manuscript pages daily for twenty-two days) had no interruption at all.

Framley Parsonage made Trollope a star novelist. Moreover, this novel, serialized from January 1860 through April 1861, changed him permanently into a serial novelist. Of the thirty-nine novels published after *Framley Parsonage*, only *Miss Mackenzie* (1865) was not intended for serial publication. Trollope believed that serial instalments had to hang together as a unit, regardless of the number of chapters they contained. This called for careful planning. His serialized novels appeared in many different configurations, sometimes improvised by the publisher, but generally under his direct control: monthly, in maga-zines or independent 'parts,' coming out in six, eight, twelve, sixteen, or twenty instalments; weekly, in magazines or 'parts,' appearing in twelve, twenty-six, thirty-two, or forty instalments. Trollope's talent for propor-tioning his work to order enabled him to write his novels to exactly prescribed limits: instalments per novel, chapters per instalment, pages per chapter, right down to words per page.

The most explicit account of this kind of working-to-order is seen in his negotiations with George Smith for the publication of *The Last Chronicle of Barset*. In early 1866 Trollope proposed a long novel in twenty shilling parts (like his own *Orley Farm*, 1861–62, itself modelled on Dickens's standard format, wherein the number of words was equiv-alent to five 'volumes' rather than the traditional three volumes in which most Victorian fiction appeared). Smith agreed, but said that he was not sure whether he would publish the book in twenty instalments or in an unusual thirty instalments. Trollope then told Smith that if the story must be written for possible division into twenty *or* thirty instal-ments, he must prepare to accommodate the dual possibilities:

> It would not be practicable to divide 20 numbers into 30 equal parts, unless the work be specially done with this intent. I commonly divide a number of 32 pages (such as the numbers of 'Orley Farm') into 4 chapters each. If you wish the work to be so arranged as to run to either 20 or to 30 numbers, I must work each of the 20 numbers by 6 chapters, taking care that the chapters run equally, two and two, as to make each four into one equal part or each six into one equal part. There will be some trouble in this, but having a mechanical mind I think I can do it ... You will understand that I wish to suit your views

altogether; but that it is necessary that you should say – Write it in 20 parts or in 30 parts – or in parts to suit either number. And you will understand that if your mind be made up either to 30 or to 20, you need not put my mechanical genius to work.

(Trollope 1983, I, 328–9)

Smith decided on twenty monthly parts, then, two days later, changed his mind and asked for thirty-two weekly parts. Trollope obliged.

The period 1860–67 was (by a slender margin) the most productive of his writing career. During these years he further cemented his connection to the 'literary life' by establishing friendships with various writers (Thackeray chief among them), by becoming a member of the Garrick Club and of the Athenaeum Club, and by taking an active role in the Royal Literary Fund (a charity that gave monetary assistance to indigent writers and their families). His reputation as a writer had risen to the top – he was labelled 'the king of serial novelists' (Dickens's production had fallen off sharply in the last decade of his life) and 'almost a national institution' (Smalley 1969, 167). His earnings from his novels had spiralled continually upward, reaching some £3000 for his copyrights.

Parallel to these successes, he also attempted to move upward in the postal service, an attempt that shows that for all this time as a novelist, from the unsuccessful Irish years to the grand triumphs of the 1860s, the Post Office had remained his chief occupation and concern. In March 1864 his old adversary Rowland Hill retired from the Secretaryship of the Post Office and his place was quickly given to the Assistant Secretary, John Tilley, Trollope's close friend and brother-in-law. Trollope then applied for Tilley's vacant Assistant Secretaryship, a post to which he felt entitled by seniority and 'special services' (his work in the West Country and postal missions to Egypt and to the West Indies). In many ways the ambition of higher office (Surveyors ranked not far below the Assistant Secretary) appears wrongheaded, or odd, to say the least. Trollope himself explained it:

Had I obtained this [promotion] I should have given up my hunting, have given up much of my literary work, – at any rate would have edited no magazine, and would have returned to the habit of my youth in going daily to the General Post Office. There was very much against such a change in life. The increase in salary would not have amounted to above £400 a year, and I should have lost much more than that in literary remuneration. I should have felt bitterly the slavery of attendance at an office, from which I had been exempt for five-and-twenty years. I should, too, have greatly missed the sport which I loved. But I was attached to the department, had imbued myself with a thorough love of letters, – I mean the letters which are carried by the post, – and was anxious for their welfare as though they were all my own. In short, I wished to continue the connexion. I did not wish, moreover, that any younger officer should again pass over my head. (Trollope 1950, 278–9)

But Tilley appointed the younger aspirant. Trollope fumed for a time. The department offered him another special mission, this time to the East, but Trollope refused. Then in 1866 he undertook another 'special service,' that of reorganizing the sorting and delivery of letters in London. For some years the metropolitan area had been divided into postal districts (the familiar W, WC, etc.) and under the supervision of one controller in the Circulation Department. Trollope was asked to submit a plan to convert eight of the ten London postal districts into individual 'postal towns.' His proposal was accepted, and he was made temporary 'surveyor' of this new 'district.' A postal employee recalled him at this work: 'I have seen him slogging away at papers at a stand-up desk, with his handkerchief stuffed into his mouth, and his hair on end, as though he could barely contain himself. He struck me as being a rather fierce-looking man' ('R.J.' 1896, 295). Trollope completed the assignment in a few months and was immediately offered the perma-nent Surveyorship of the Metropolitan District, but he declined. By this time, he had determined to retire from the service. On 2 October 1867, having given thirty-three years of his life to the Post Office, Trollope sent in his resignation. It occasioned a generous letter from the Secre-tary, thanking him for his service, and calling him 'one of the most conspicuous servants of the Post Office.' The letter added that Trollope had never allowed 'other avocations' to interfere with his official work, 'which has always been performed faithfully, and indeed energetically.' Trollope said that the word 'energetically' did not, even with its 'touch of irony,' displease him; he reprinted the entire letter in An Autobiog-raphy as evidence that he did not allow his literary labours to interfere with his postal work (Trollope 1950, 280–1).

His face has never been on a postage stamp. The excuse given in 1993, when Trollope was commemorated with a stone in Poets' Corner in Westminster Abbey, was that such honours are bestowed only during anniversary years. Perhaps 2015 – or 2082 – will see him so commemo-rated.

1867–1882

In 'retirement' Trollope worked continuously and doggedly. He remained for three years as editor of his own unsuccessful *St. Paul's Magazine*. In 1871 he moved out of Waltham Cross on the occasion of an eighteen-month visit to his son in Australia (and the occasion of huge books on Australia and New Zealand). On arriving back in England he took a house in the heart of London, at 39 Montagu Square, where he intended to live out his life. But in due course he and his wife tired of the city, and in May 1880 removed to the country at South Harting, near Petersfield, whence Trollope came regularly into London and stayed at Garlant's Hotel in Suffolk Street.

Although one might have expected his writing productivity to increase in retirement, he wrote slightly, just a tad, less than while engaged in two professions. He said that three hours a day of writing (four on the right kind of holiday) was about all that one could do anyway, so retirement had little effect on his output. But he continued to write: novels, two huge travel books, biographies, and articles.

We have little evidence of his precise working conditions in retirement. It may be presumed that he altered his early-rising routine. Certainly he did so later in life. By the autumn of 1878 he had developed a bad case of writer's cramp, and he dictated about a third of a short novel, *Cousin Henry*, to Florence Bland, his wife's niece (who for all practical purposes had been his adopted daughter since 1863). She would continue to serve as his amanuensis until the end, and in time would take down as much as two-thirds of some of his late manuscripts. These manuscripts show his and Florence's hand alternating according to no pattern. He would frequently begin a chapter but give over after a page or a paragraph. Sometimes the hands change in mid-paragraph, even in mid-sentence. Given Trollope's concentration and impatience, it must have been trying work for the young woman. According to one friend, Florence was forbidden to make the slightest suggestion or comment during the writing sessions, and on one occasion when she did 'a whole chapter was consigned to the waste-paper basket' (Meetkerke 1883, 317).

He needed quiet to write, and Montagu Square did not always provide it; there,

> Of all the nuisances ... noises are the worst ... To think with a barrel organ within hearing is heroic. For myself, I own that a brass band altogether incapacitates me. No sooner does the first note of the

opening burst reach my ear, than I start up, fling down my pen, and cast my thoughts disregarded into the abyss of some chaos which is always there ready to receive them. (Trollope 1981, 2)

Indeed, on 3 November 1882, while resident and working at Garlant's Hotel in London, the day on which he was stricken with the stroke from which he would die a month later, he had an altercation with the leader of a German street band playing outside his window.[5] His death left the novel he had in hand, *The Landleaguers*, unfinished. In his desk drawer were two complete manuscripts; that of the novel *An Old Man's Love* and that of *An Autobiography*.

How did he do it?

Trollope himself would have said that all the talk of early rising, working diaries, writing while travelling, and so on leaves out the essential element in his novel writing. It started back in his miserable time at Winchester when young Anthony, then about twelve years of age, developed the habit of escaping from his troubles, failures, and lack of companionship into an imaginary world. As a boy, and even a child, he had been often thrown upon himself. Other boys had not much played with him, and he had had to 'form my play within myself.' The practice became continuous, almost systematic:

Study was not my bent, and I could not please myself by being all idle. Thus it came to pass that I was always going about with some castle in the air firmly built within my mind. Nor were these efforts in architecture spasmodic, or subject to constant change from day to day. For weeks, for months, if I remember rightly, from year to year, I would carry on the same tale binding myself down to certain laws, to certain proportions, and proprieties, and unities. Nothing impossible was ever introduced, – nor anything which, from outward circumstances' would seem to be violently improbable. I myself was of course my own hero. Such is the necessity of castle building. But I never became a king, or a duke, – much less when my height and personal appearance were fixed could I be an Antinous, or six feet high. I never was a learned man, nor even a philosopher. But I was

[5]   This account comes from Michael Sadleir, who may have heard it from Trollope's son (Sadleir 1961, 331). That it sounds suspiciously like Trollope's own account of his Montagu Square troubles need not necessarily invalidate it.

a very clever person, and beautiful young women used to be fond of me. And I strove to be kind of heart, and open of hand, and noble in thought, despising mean things; and altogether I was a very much better fellow that I have ever succeeded in being since. This had been the occupation of my life for six or seven years before I went to the Post Office, and was by no means abandoned when I commenced my work. There can, I imagine, hardly be a more dangerous mental practice; but I have often doubted whether, had it not been my practice, I should ever have written a novel. I learned in this way to maintain an interest in a fictitious story, to dwell on a work created by my own imagination, and to live in a world altogether outside the world of my material life. In after years I have done the same, – with this difference, that I have discarded the hero of my early dreams, and have been able to lay my own identity aside.

(Trollope 1950, 42–3)

An additional source of Trollope's writing habits can be discovered in a short story called 'The Panjandrum' written in 1870 for his own *St. Paul's Magazine* and published in a book of short stories, *An Editor's Tales*, in June of the same year. In *An Autobiography* Trollope described the story as having its roots 'in my own early days ... over an abortive periodical which was intended to be the finest thing ever done' (Trollope 1950, 337). The setting for the story is 1840–41, the final years of his unhappy Post Office clerkship. The narrator is one of six 'impoverished' people who determine to bring out their own magazine, to be called *The Panjandrum*. The story's narrator, plainly meant to be Trollope himself, age twenty-five, is chosen as editor. He prepares a short story for the first editorial meeting – at which time everyone is entirely dissatisfied with everyone else's would-be contribution, and the plan for founding a magazine is abandoned.

Trollope's story is chiefly about how the narrator came to write his story. It is a detailed account of how his 'day dreaming' and 'castle building' emerged into fiction. One cannot determine today whether he actually wrote a story at the time, or whether he is merely reflecting on his later method. The young would-be writer, while walking in Regent's Park on a harsh, rainy day, sees a middle-aged servant woman leading a girl of ten or eleven with mud all over her stockings. As he passes them, the girl says, 'Oh, Anne, I do so wonder what he's like!' Anne tells her, 'You'll see.' The narrator begins thinking: who is it that the girl comes 'tripping along through the rain and mud to see, and kiss, and love, and wonder at? And why hadn't she been taken in a cab? Would she be allowed to take off those dirty stockings before she was introduced to

her new-found brother, or wrapped in the arms of her stranger father?'
The aspiring writer saw no more of the girl and servant, but 'thought a
great deal of the girl.' 'Gradually,' we are told, 'as the unforced imagination came to play upon the matter, a little picture fashioned itself in my
mind.' Walking the whole round of Regent's Park, he builds his castle
in the air, a story called 'The New Inmate.' 'The girl was my own sister,
– a sister whom I had never seen till she was thus brought to me for
protection and love; but she was older, just budding into womanhood.'
He furnishes a little white-curtained sitting-room, provides her with
books, a piano, a low sofa, and 'all little feminine belongings.' He sells
his horse ('the horse of my imagination, the reader will understand, for I
had never in truth possessed such an animal'), resigns from his club, and
devotes himself to taking care of his sister. But she soon falls in love and
is given in marriage to his friend Walker. The narrator, returning home
out of the rain, cannot wait to take up his pen. For five days he works
on the story. When not writing, while 'walking, eating, or reading,' he
thinks of the story. He dreams of it, weeps over it. The story becomes 'a
matter that admitted no doubt'; the little girl with the muddy stockings
is but a 'blessed memory,' while his new-found sister is 'palpably' real.

> All her sweetnesses were present to me, as though I had her there,
> in the little turning out of Theobald's Road. To this moment I can
> distinguish the voice in which she spoke to me that little whispered
> word, when I asked whether she cared for Walker. When one thinks
> of it, the reality of it all is appalling. What need is there of a sister
> or a friend in the flesh ... when by a little exercise of the mind they
> may be there at your elbow, faultless? (Trollope 1870, 213)

And so it seems that when, in An Autobiography, Trollope describes
himself as 'living with his characters,' and 'weeping with them, laughing
with them,' when he says he lived ever with the ghost of Mrs Proudie
after killing her off in The Last Chronicle, he was not speaking altogether figuratively. (His claim reminds one of the stir G. H. Lewes
caused when he wrote that Dickens had told him that he 'heard' every
word his characters spoke.) Trollope's fictional characters came to take
on an 'appalling reality' for him. He wrote of Phineas Redux:

> So much of my inner life was passed in their company [Plantagenet
> Palliser, Lady Glencora, the old Duke of Omnium, Phineas Finn,
> Lady Laura, Violet Effingham, and Madame Max Goesler] that I
> was continually asking myself how this woman would act when this
> or that event had passed over her head, or how that man would

carry himself when his youth had become manhood, or his manhood declined to old age ... As to the incidents of the story, the circumstances by which these personages were to be affected, I knew nothing. They were created for the most part as they were described. I never could arrange a set of events before me. But the evil and the good of my puppets, and how the evil would always lead to evil, and the good produce good, – that was clear to me as are the stars on a summer night. (Trollope 1950, 319–20)

Moreover, some of his fictional characters were becoming 'real' to his readers as well. When Trollope ended the Barchester Series with *The Last Chronicle*, R. H. Hutton, one of the shrewdest of Victorian reviewers, quotes a friend as saying that Archdeacon Grantly 'was one of my best and most intimate friends. It was bad enough to lose the Old Warden, Mr Septimus Harding, but that was a natural death ... Mr Trollope has no right to break old ties in this cruel and reckless way.' Mrs Oliphant, in *Blackwood's Magazine*, wrote, 'We did not ask that this Chronicle should be the last. We were in no hurry to be done with our old friends ... To kill Mrs Proudie was murder, or manslaughter at the least' (Smalley 1969, 291, 303–4). Virginia Woolf said that we believe in Trollope's characters 'as we do in the reality of our weekly bills,' and that we get from his novels 'the same sort of refreshment and delight that we get from seeing something actually happen in the street below' (Woolf 1967, 57, 62).

Late in life, on holiday with his wife, Trollope found the Black Forest and the mountains of Switzerland especially conducive to his 'castle building.' In an article, 'A Walk in a Wood,' published in *Good Words* in 1879, he dilated upon how for him the most difficult part of creating a novel was not the actual writing, but the thinking, that 'elbow grease of the mind' that had to be done preliminary to putting pen to paper. By this, he explains, he did not mean thinking about the 'entire plot' or overall story since the larger incidents of his tales 'are fabricated to fit my story as it goes on, and not my story to fit the incidents.' (He mentions Lady Mason's confessing her forgery, Mrs Proudie's dying of a heart attack, and Lizzie Eustace's stealing her own diamonds as examples of large plot developments that had come upon him suddenly in the midst of working on a novel.) Rather, the hard work of thinking was expended on the 'minute ramifications of tale-telling, – how this young lady should be made to behave herself with that young gentleman; – how this mother or that father would be affected by the ill conduct or the good of a son or a daughter.' Such thinking, Trollope goes on, is best served by peaceful surroundings:

> Bad noises, bad air, bad smells, bad light, an inconvenient attitude, ugly surroundings, little misfortunes that have lately been endured, little misfortunes that are soon to come, hunger and thirst, overeating and overdrinking, want of sleep or too much of it, a tight boot, a starched collar, are all inimical to thinking ... It is not the sorrows but the annoyances of life which impede. Were I told that the bank had broken in which my little all was kept for me I could sit down and write my love story ... but to discover that I had given half a sovereign instead of sixpence to a cabman would render a great effort necessary before I could find the fitting words for a lover. These little lacerations of the spirit, not the deep wounds, make the difficulty.

Although he could do some of this 'thinking' in a carriage (not in a railway carriage – though he could write in one) and even on horseback, he much preferred to do the work while walking in a wood. It is best, he writes, to reject even the company of a dog, and to keep away from cottages, children, and chance wanderers, 'so much easier it is to speak than to think.' The 'pure forests' of Switzerland and the Black Forest were the perfect 'hunting grounds for thought' (Trollope 1981, 595–9).

But this walking in a wood was on holiday and very late in his life. How he found time in other circumstances for 'thinking about his characters' continues to intrigue his admirers. He was writing with, if anything, great productivity when he was employed in the Post Office, travelling continuously in his work (his 'principal occupation'), but also hunting, playing cards, studying the classics, reading systematically hundreds of Elizabethan and Jacobean plays, writing travel books and biographies, articles and reviews for magazines. We have not mentioned correcting proofs.

How did he do it? Unusual physical stamina, extraordinary powers of concentration, the ability to give his entire being, body and mind, to the task in hand, an uncanny verbal memory, methodical working habits strenuously and stubbornly abided by, a down-to-earth relish of monetary rewards, an ambition for the 'charms of reputation ... I wished from the beginning to be something more than a clerk in a Post Office. To be known as somebody, – to be Anthony Trollope if it be no more, – is to me much' (Trollope 1950, 107). If these explanations fall short, I offer one given me by a graduate student to whom the working diary was shown. She said, 'He's not human.' It's a thought.

Works Cited

Bradley, Edward ('Cuthbert Bede'), 1882. 'Some Recollections of Mr Anthony Trollope,' *Graphic*, 26 (23 December 1882): 707–8.

Escott, T. H. S., 1913. *Anthony Trollope: His Work, Associates, and Literary Originals*. London: John Lane.

Harrison, Frederic, 1895. *Studies in Early Victorian Literature*. London: Edward Arnold.

[Meetkerke, Cecilia,] 1883. 'Anthony Trollope,' *Blackwood's Magazine*, 133 (February 1883): 315–21.

[Morley, John, and Mrs Humphry Ward], 1883. 'Anthony Trollope,' *Macmillan's Magazine*, 49 (November 1883): 51–61.

R.J., 1896. 'Early Post Office Days,' *St Martin's-le-Grand* (July 1896): 293–6.

Sadleir, Michael, 1961. *Trollope: A Commentary* (1927). London: Oxford University Press.

Smalley, Donald, 1969. *Trollope: The Critical Heritage*. London: Routledge & Kegan Paul.

Trollope, Anthony, 1870. *An Editor's Tales*. London: Strahan.

Trollope, Anthony, 1879. *Thackeray*. London: Macmillan.

Trollope, Anthony, 1950. *An Autobiography* (1883). London: Oxford University Press.

Trollope, Anthony, 1981. 'A Walk in a Wood,' *Good Words*, 20 (September 1879): 595–9.

Trollope, Anthony, 1983. *The Letters of Anthony Trollope*, ed. N. John Hall. 2 vols. Stanford: Stanford University Press.

Woolf, Virginia, 1967. 'Phases of Fiction,' in *Collected Essays II*. New York: Harcourt, Brace, & World.

Literary Netscapes: Web Poetry and Blogging

GRAEME HARPER interviews ROBERT SHEPPARD

GH: Can we start with how your print magazine, *Pages* [begun in 1987], became a blog in February 2005?

RS: I'd coined the term 'blogzine' (only to find Martin Stannard had been there before me, with 'blog-zine') to imply I was appropriating a modern technology for a little magazine (much as previous generations had borrowed office technologies such as the duplicator and photo-copier). It was all quite modest: I carried over the title of *Pages* (and the pagination, with some difficulty) to www.robertsheppard.blogspot.com, to start its third series.

GH: What happened?

RS: The print magazine had been quietly influential, not least in promoting the ugly term 'linguistically innovative poetry,' by providing the first use of the words (by Gilbert Adair) and by presenting poetry, essays and poets' statements under a 'resources for the linguistically innovative poetries' strapline in series two. In the third – the Web – series that last resources aspect was important to me. At first the zine half dominated, where my critical offcuts were juxtaposed with the poetry and prose of others, from Iain Sinclair and Bill Griffiths to newcomers like Dee McMahon and Alice Lenkiewicz. For instance, in the Poetry Buzz event for Allen Fisher's sixtieth birthday, I posted photos of the day and used them as illustrations for postings of work by performers from that day: readings for Allen at three locations in London, and on board the poetry bus that transported us. All very communal and under the shadow of the July 2005 bombings in London too.

Then Mr Hyde's blog-like influence took over, as I began to present not just bits and pieces of critical books I was working on, but also entries about my being fifty or reading 'Smokestack Lightning' to a friend's blues band. I discovered early on that the 'send a comment' facility was immediately filled with spam, so I had to block that, unfortunately. I realized the process of editing and posting could go on forever. It all became less of a virtual discussion and turned into a blog. So I stopped it.

GH: What's happened, then, in the current fourth series?

RS: It's going to be strictly answers to one simple question: what's been going on in alternative forms of British poetry since 2000? My first 'reply' is not a reply at all, it's an edited version of a contribution by Salt Publishing's Chris Hamilton-Emery to an email discussion list. That's where virtual discussion is meant to happen, isn't it? But it seldom does. In the early days of the British Poets' list, say 1997 for example, critics like Marjorie Perloff and poets like John Wilkinson posted splendid mini-essays. But at some point they left off, perhaps disenchanted with the medium or its processes. Disenchantment set in for me when I realized that the same argument had started up for a second time; the list's open-endedness offered no conclusion, its supposedly linear 'strands' caught in some cyber-eternal return – a little like blogs themselves. Coming back to *Pages*, I decided to post answers to that one crucial question, one I don't know the answer to, but whose answers will prove to be a resource for the future. Already Adrian Clarke's characteristically abrasive response to Hamilton-Emery has injected some fire into the exchange.

GH: As both poet and critic, how do you use the creative space of the blog?

RS: I haven't theorized the use of webspace, but, basically, I see a simple tool not a democratized informational utopia. One of the private functions of *Pages* was to teach myself to read poetry on screen. I can't – but I think my students can. I decided to publish on the Web on seeing how readily my students used it to access poems and poetry information. I also found the production of links very liberating, particularly where I was drawing together a virtual collection of my work by merely pointing to its locations. Linkage is part of my poetics, and it's in the structure of my *Twentieth Century Blues* (a pseudo-hyperlink of seventy-five titles and dozens of interrelated strands of sub-titles!). I enjoyed posting disguised parts of critical books too: criticism should exist as a critical space *within* the poetry world, in order to affect it, not just reflect it. Finally, I want to diminish the blog aspect, all that instant opinion or even trivia that dominates the medium (or is it now a genre?).

GH: There's an interesting comment you make online about the mainstream not being a 'binary opposition of the avant-garde'.

RS: There's a theoretical distinction, influenced by Levinas, between a poetry of the said and a poetry of saying, the first of ontological violence and closure, the second of ineffable openness in eternality. The two aren't a binary, since the open-endedness of the saying can only be embodied in the fixity of the said. My unease with the blog and the nature of discussion lists can be seen through those Levinasian lenses: the unending saying of the cyber-discussion *needs* the fixity (even violence) of the said of conclusiveness and closure, perhaps, but technologically and experientially the media lack that. Imagine the horror of a poem that would speak itself forever! Or a blog that would last a thousand years, with teams of dynastic neophytes trained up for the job.

GH: Using your blog as a sounding board, what do you think are the most significant developments in contemporary British and Irish poetry?

RS: This is the very question I am posing my *Pages* contributors! I don't know the answer, but I suspect that within 'linguistically innovative poetry' the influence of the Performance Writing course that John Hall and Caroline Bergvall set up at Dartington College of the Arts is widespread, particularly through a dispersal of its staff and graduates nationwide: Mark Leahy, Dell Olsen, and others. Their expanded sense of the performative and visual aspects of language has revived an interest in (old) concrete poetry but also in (new) cyber- and Web-based works: the two strands that meet utterly in the work of Maggie O'Sullivan, for example. There is a visually oriented audience out there, partly because one can use the Web so easily. Print-on-demand technologies and selling books over the Web (the Salt and Shearsman approach) have made publication easier. This has led to the production of major collected poems, for instance, by John James, Lee Harwood, David Chaloner, which allows us to investigate as a whole the *oeuvres* of major veteran figures in this scene, and rewrite our histories.

GH: What's your view on archiving blogs?

RS: A blog archives itself, doesn't it – which is deceptive. I was talking to Los Glazier about the marvellous Electronic Poetry Center at Buffalo, and he said that the university which hosts it could pull the plug at any moment. The same could happen with any blog, but we behave as if it won't. Look at all the links on *Pages* that are dead-ends. The poetry audio archive begun by Andrea Brady is a superb resource for the future with a suggestive and relevant name: The Archive of the Now. We've got to save that 'now' before it becomes a vanished 'then'.

GH: Your blog identity is out of date, so has the blog taken over and the writer's real presence disappeared?

RS: Cyber-ageing is an accelerated process, and cyber-space junk litters the blogosphere. What will it look like in ten years time? Even if identity is only the shadow of existence, too much of me was appearing on my blog! But the me that is left is probably the me of 2005–6, when I was most furiously posting the blog. Series four won't involve me at all.

GH: Do you think the blog has an effect on your creative and critical writing?

RS: Very minor. For me, it's a tool, not a writing technology. I thought maybe I could use the colour facility to write specifically for the blog (I was looking at Jacques Roubaud's multi-coloured and multi-voiced *Kyrielle*) but I never did. It was too difficult to format and indent and so on, and anyway I had those doubts about people like me not being able to read poetry online. That's one reason for the fourth series being prose. The editor of the poetry Web magazine *Jacket*, John Tranter, says: don't send me stuff with indents and crazy typefaces, I can't handle it, and I don't like it anyway.

GH: What about the critical work?

RS: *Pages* blogzine was meant to be a relief from the academic world, and a re-connection with my primary creative environment. It was supposed to come from within the creative environment, not outside it. But the blog was cited in the entry for my university's Research Assessment Exercise, much against my will.

GH: Your thoughts on the creative environment of contemporary British poetry?

RS: A key issue here – that Web publishing can address – is the environment of reception. Just a wider range of poets being heard of and read. Around the millennium there was a spate of critical works and anthologies which announced a true democracy in British verse. They kow-towed to various correctnesses: the end of the poetry wars, that sort of thing. However, despite the consensual rhetoric, these antholo-gies completely left out most of the writers in whom I am interested – including some of those I've named here – and the various crea-tive environments that have sustained them, their reading series, their publishers. Beware the commentators who declare their catholicity while operating according to secret proscriptions. Better the opposi-tional openness of somebody like Don Paterson.

GH: Finally, confronted with the term 'creative environment,' what springs to mind?

RS: Concentric circles outside (and inside) the writer, of activities and support systems. What Bourdieu calls the field of cultural production, I suppose. Some parts are obvious: publishing, reviews, time, peers, creative-writing workshops even. Others are less obvious: poetry read-ings, your Mum, bars of chocolate, mugs of coffee. Then there are the sustaining networks of communication. Blogs – zines or not, one's own or others – can be part of that.

There are negative circles too: time, a lack of appreciation of the work by critics, peers, and – just as important – employer, family, and the cat, reticence, bad habits. John Hall's essay 'Writing and Not Writing' (in Denise Riley's *Poets on Writing*, 1992) is partly about the loss of his crea-tive environment. Extrinsic economic necessity and intrinsic absorp-tion in teaching squeezed out modalities of his writing, which turned into dull reportage or professional writing. It's a limit case of poetics, a gentle horror story. However, it has a happy and instructive ending: Hall later returned to writing a different poetry by being involved in the deliberate development of a new creative environment at Dartington College of the Arts mentioned earlier, where he was Principal.

Growing Up and Zoning Out:
Charlotte and Emily Brontë

STEVIE DAVIES

Now

FOUR NOVELISTS – three women and one man – are gathered in the library at the Brontë Parsonage Museum at Haworth, bending over a lectern on which is displayed the tiniest imaginable manuscript. With white-gloved hands, the Arts Director, Ann Dinsdale, shows the writers one of the minuscule books made by the Brontë siblings in their childhood. Nobody speaks. We all bend our faces nearer to the script, passionately curious to make out the writing. But at this distance and without a magnifying glass, it is indecipherable.

'These books were made, don't forget, for the toy soldiers to read,' Ann reminds us, explaining that the book, the September issue of 'Blackwood's Young Men's Magazine,' had been written by Charlotte and bound up between 20 August and 25 August 1829. Leafing through, she shows us the contents page and advertisements, prose and poetry, hand-sewn into rough brown paper covers. There are sixteen leaves; the book, incredibly, measures thirty-six by fifty-five millimetres. Acquired by Charlotte's publisher, George Smith (presumably at one of the Nicholls sales held at Sotheby's), it passed to his granddaughter and was bequeathed to the Brontë Parsonage Museum in 1975. We are mesmerized by the thought of the prodigious labour undertaken to produce these hundreds of thousands of words, generated in a script illegible to father or aunt, using recycled materials that testify to the economies of a thrifty household. The tiny books were constructed of scraps of paper sewn into covers made from odd bits of sugar bags, parcel wrappings, wallpaper.

'Where are the toy soldiers? May we see them?' asks Toby Litt, author of a book entitled, with singular aptness, *deadkidsongs*. But the wooden soldiers, originally gifts to Branwell, disintegrated under the ferocity of the children's games that took place in every gore-soaked room in the house, from the cellar (serving as a prison) to the heath above the Parsonage, where campaigns warlike and imperialist were waged. Branwell, the only boy, had received three sets of soldiers from Bradford,

Keighley, and Leeds. 'The Twelves' were the basis for the characters of the Brontë fictional world, initiating a series of 'plays,' the Young Men's Plays, Our Fellows, The Islanders, as well as games between Emily and Charlotte, 'bed plays' – 'all our plays,' wrote Charlotte, 'are very strange ones.' Branwell recorded that he had 'Maimed Lost burnt or destroyed' two dozen toy soldiers during the year of his sisters' absence at Cowan Bridge (Barker 1994, 116).

As we four visiting novelists, nearly one hundred and eighty years later, marvel at the minute 'Brontë small script,' we have the sensation of looking over the shoulders of those wildly imaginative and piercingly intelligent children in the act of creating a fictional world that would change our literature forever. The motherless children did this in the shadow of their elder sisters' recent deaths. Because this is a private viewing, we have the Parsonage (generally milling with a crush of visitors) to ourselves, sharing intimate space with authors who have been part of our lives since childhood.

Then

Such continuity of print and leaf through time was pondered by the Brontës at an early age. In March 1829, Charlotte is sitting in the kitchen, with a book.

> Once papa lent my Sister Maria A Book it was an old Geography and she wrote on it[s] Blank leaf papa lent me this Book. the Book is an hundred and twenty years old[.] it is at this moment lying Before me while I write this [.] I am in the kitchin of the parsonage house Hawarth[.] Taby the servent is washing up after Breakfast and Anne my youngest Sister (Maria was my eldest) is kneeling on a chair looking at some cakes. ... Our plays were established Young Men June 1826 Our fellows July 1827 islanders December 1827
> (C. Brontë 1996, 2)

A treasured book is passed from hand to hand. Returned to its owner, it carries the borrower's ghostly fingerprint, the signature of Maria, on an inviting blank page. The child dies. Book and inscription remain. A bereaved younger child, now the family's eldest, takes her place. Her eyes, like those of her dead sister, consider the provenance of the book, marvelling at its vintage. The warm, quotidian life of the Parsonage continues around Charlotte. She locates each member of her family in the present moment, her father and brother having gone for the newspapers, which she lists and describes, adding that a friend lends the family 'Blackwoods Magazine the most able periodical there is.' The issue of 'Blackwood's Young Men's Magazine' shown to us in the library is one in a series created in emulation of that magazine, edited first by Branwell, then (when he got tired of it) by Charlotte. The little book, which we all now somehow consider to be 'ours,' is linked to twin domains: to education and to play. Precious adult reading matter (the world as it is held to be) is imaginatively transformed, through child's play, into the world as they would like it to be. Charlotte describes creative context and conception. The book Maria signed and Charlotte turns over in her hands is 'an hundred and twenty years old.' Meanwhile the manuscript book we study in 2008 is venerable. Not only does it carry visual traces of its author, editor, publisher, and printer – the nearly thirteen-year-old Charlotte – but it does so in such a fresh, exuberant manner that it seems to have been created yesterday.

Minuscule as they are, these manuscripts boast a limitless ambition, for 'Brontë small script' was devised to emulate print and mimic publication. It was nothing like the copybook cursive script children were taught, where the aim was to produce a handwriting that was elegant, slanted, regular and flowing – and above all, legible. In an age before the typewriter, no version of a 'printed' and reproduced effect was available in the personal realm. So the children crafted it themselves. The girls enjoyed a liberty unusual in genteel households: any book in the house they wished to read was theirs. This licit private reading was a breakout, giving entry to a culture generally forbidden to women. Open a book used by the young Brontës and it seems to burst out into a 'great crack o' laughing,' with subversive doodles on its margins and endpapers or the names of fictional places inscribed in a geography book. Their father was also a vehement scribbler in margins. Marginalia are a form of extemporized private assertion that challenges the centre for priority. The Brontë girls were in some ways honorary boys.

The soldiers for whose eyes the little books were created marched into the Parsonage on 5 June 1826. Charlotte records their advent thus:

> papa bought Branwell some soldiers at Leeds when papa came home it was night and we where in Bed so next morning Branwell came to our Door with a Box of soldiers Emily and I jumped out of Bed and I snat[c]hed up one and exclaimed this is the Duke of Wellington it shall be mine!! when I said this Emily likewise took one and said it should be hers when Anne came down she took one also. Mine

was the prettiest of the whole and perfect in every part Emilys was a
Grave looking fellow we called him Gravey Anne's was a queer little
thing very much like herself. he was called waiting Boy Branwell
chose Bonaparte (Barker 1994, 154)

What Charlotte remembered as a snatch-and-grab raid, Branwell
recalled as a two-stage legitimate allocation: 'to take care of them
though they were to be mine and I to have the disposal of them as I
would – shortly after this I gave them to them as their own' (Barker
1994, 864). By this time, the children had generated so many pseu-
donyms and pseudonymous nicknames that the air was thick with
multiple personalities. All – so far – male.

At what point did the game become a form of proto-workshop,
with its own agreed back story forming a basis for all subsequent
development of multiple plots and characters? Childhood games are
pure performance, a power grab. The home becomes theatrical space,
children actors. At first the four children composed together, before
splitting into two groups. The Young Men's plays lasted Branwell and
Charlotte, the older writing pair, for twenty years. The younger Emily
and Anne were originally dealt lower caste soldiers, with less mega-
lomaniac designations. Branwell-Bonaparte and Charlotte-Wellington
stride like colossi around the fictional world, but Emily's man is commu-
nally named for his comic reflection of her expression ('Gravey') and to
Anne – a funny-faced person of six – is granted an odd little bod named
'Waiting Boy.' The older children patronized and scorned the younger.
In 'A Day at Parry's Palace,' Charlotte mocked the little girls' imaginative paucity: rather than soldiers, their characters are dolls, the dialogue
either uncouth muttering, baby-talk or nothing whatever. Emily's and
Anne's idea of high architecture is a kind of working farm, with stone
pumpkins for decoration. The visiting Charles Wellesley, addled with
boredom, assaults the gurning babe, Eater, with a poker and kicks him,
'hoping to stun him' into silence (C. Brontë 1996, 97). Branwell's 'chief
man,' Bonaparte, was to be joined by other personae, notably Sneaky
and Rogue, ultimately morphing into the romantic aristocrat, North-
angerland.

In *Blackwood's Magazine*, the children had read of Britain's imperialist adventure in Africa. Their soldiers were veterans of the Duke of
Wellington's army who, having fought campaigns through Portugal and
Spain in the Peninsular War (1808–14), now embarked on an African
campaign, founding a colony in the kingdom of Ashantee, represented
by a set of ninepins. The toy soldiers persecuted the enslaved black

community in four lands – Wellingtonsland, Sneakysland, Parrysland, and Rossesland. Their capitals were called Glasstowns. From these colonies, with their aggressive imperialist assumptions, developed Angria and Gondal. At this stage, most of their people were male, their ethic military and patriarchal. After all, female soldiers and politicians did not at that era exist – except metaphorically at kitchen tables where subversive daughters gave cheeky answers and wrote their way into a life of power and agency. Queen Victoria's ascent to the throne in 1837 would be eagerly noted by the sisters.

The simplicity of the Brontë home reminds us of the family's relatively austere living conditions: stone-flagged and chiefly carpetless ground-floor rooms, uncurtained windows, in a working-class manufacturing town. The mills lay in the valley, while their father's Church of St Michael and All Angels surmounted the steep cobbled hill, Main Street. Labourers crowded together in insanitary terraced cottages; their dead in the graveyard of Mr Brontë's church leaked putrescence into the water system. Beyond the Parsonage lay the open moors. The fierce cold of a northern winter was opposed by roaring fires in the Parsonage grate: but the outside seemed all too near the inside. Reading the Brontë fiction, we are aware of living spaces, intensely realized: thin partitions bound the solitary individual's interior space. At the opening of *Jane Eyre*, Jane reads in a window seat at Gateshead, separated by a pane from the storm outside, a red moreen curtain screening her from her cousin's violence. Asylum, signified by enough to eat, a safe room, and a banked-up fire, is always endangered and ephemeral. Indoor and outdoor worlds, linked and separated by a membrane, are riddlingly connected. In *Wuthering Heights*, itself fashioned like a nest of Russian dolls, Catherine's box bed, the inside of the inside, gives on to the stormy outdoor world through a glass pane whose transparency haunts the sleeper with dreams of dead and wandering children.

Outside the Parsonage, and always on view when the shutters were opened, lay the graveyard, with its raised grey slabs. The children's creativity in their safe space was shadowed by trauma. Mother-loss, endured in early childhood, was compounded by the suffering of the two elder sisters, Maria and Elizabeth, brought home by their father from the Clergy Daughters' School at Cowan Bridge to die in 1825. They had stood to the youngest children in a maternal posture. Leaving home would always seem perilous to the survivors. Huddling together, they crowded their home-space with a constantly enlarging family of imaginary people, all bearing the Brontë family resemblance. As 'Little King' and 'Little Queens' and 'Chief Genii,' the players brought magical powers to bear, 'making alive again' dead characters. The exuberance of the children's creativity belonged to a wounded house. Characters in the sisters' novels would always inhabit this risky edge, a marginal position not only in the social world – governesses in elite households, exogamous marriages, women in a men's world – but also an existential threshold between life and death, nature and culture.

In the nineteenth-century world nature and culture stood closer; the artefact palpably nearer to source. The children whose dextrous fingers stitched books from scraps of paper bag also wrote with quill pens. In the 1840s, modern technology would make metal 'dip pens' the norm for Victorians; Charlotte's desk contains one quill pen and 114 steel nibs produced by a wide range of manufacturers (principally from Caldwell, Lloyd & Co.), designed to fit the wooden-shafted pen that was introduced in the 1840s. But in the 1820s and 1830s, when the children learned to write, and always to some degree thereafter, they used quills, two of which are visible in Emily's sketch of herself and Anne composing their diary paper at the drawing-room table on 26 June 1837. The sisters' fair hand, including that of the generally messy Emily, was fine and regular. Their ink was sepia-coloured gall ink, made of the tannin from oak and nut trees, or Indian ink if they could get it. Quills were produced from the stiff-spined flight feathers of geese, crows, or even turkeys. The soft down near the tip was plucked away and the barbs removed to create a grip.

Out on the moors the Brontës gleaned feathers from lapwings and ousels, visited nests, and observed the lives and deaths of wild creatures, feelingly. They felt for their calamities and witnessed man's predations. In *Wuthering Heights* Cathy undoes a pillow in the tragic scene in which she confronts her loss of Heathcliff, in a world of loss. She eviscerates the pillow, 'pulling the feathers from the rents she had just made … ranging them on the sheet according to their different species':

> 'That's a turkey's,' she murmured to herself; 'and this is a wild-duck's; and this is a pigeon's … And here is a moorcock's; and this – I should know it among a thousand – it's a lapwing's. Bonny bird; wheeling over our heads in the middle of the moor. It wanted to get to its nest … we saw its nest in the winter, full of little skeletons … Did he shoot my lapwings, Nelly. Are they red, any of them? Let me look.' (122–3)

This perception that the world of culture is created by the death of other sentient beings gives *Wuthering Heights* something of its alarming insight. The novel positions culture as artifice, pitting the Linton gentry elegance, education, magistracy, and relative luxury against the unmediated emotion, affinities, and compulsions of nature, the Heights, and the animal world. The birds whose home is the moor, the outside world, are not solely symbolic. Their lives are prized and their deaths mourned as fellow creatures. The competition of species (figured in Heathcliff's trap for the lapwings) challenges social assumptions, and makes no reference to Christian theology. 'Nature,' Emily wrote in a Brussels essay of 1842, 'The Butterfly,' 'is an inexplicable problem; it exists on a principle of destruction. Every being must be the tireless instrument of death to others, or else itself cease to live' (C. and E. Brontë, 1996, 177). What can be done about this? Nothing but 'turn the holes towards the mattress,' as Nelly does with the pillow, whose rifled bowels expose a social lie.

Like quill and feather, light and bindings also witness to a link between creative human life and creaturely death. Tapers were made of reeking tallow, candles of beeswax. When Lockwood dozes in Cathy's bed, he is awoken not by a ghost but by 'an odour of roasted calf,' his candle wick having kindled the cover of a mildewed book on the window ledge (18). Leather bindings originated in dismembered animal lives. Writing at the kitchen or drawing-room table or with portable desks on their laps, the Brontës sat closer to nature than we do and they had pondered the implications of this proximity.

How anomalous were the creative circumstances of the Brontë children? In Charlotte's play satirizing Branwell, *The Poetaster* (1830), her hero, Captain Tree, having kicked the prolix hack, Branwell-Ryhmer (sic), out of the room, laments the proliferation of poets in these latter days: 'perhaps these eyes will see through the mists of age every child that walks along the streets bearing its MSS in its hand going to the printer's for publication' (C. Brontë 1996, 88–9). Invented fantasy kingdoms, with their characters, houses, and histories, were common in an age when mass entertainment was not provided. Catherine Winkworth, the hymnographer, who became Charlotte's friend in later life, belonged to a family of prodigies. They lived in Manchester and were tutored by Elizabeth Gaskell's husband. The four Winkworth children learned to read 'long before we were four years old.' In a Calvinist household, they were permitted very few novels and fairy tales. But unrationed travel books and history stimulated their imaginations.

We lived in a whole realm of fairyland. ... There were fairies of each element, in whom, moreover, we half believed, though consciously the creatures of our own invention ... each of the four children had a Continent and a kingdom of Natural History, each choosing their representative beast as 'king' of the animals.

(Winkworth 1908, 9–10)

Catherine Winkworth invented 'expeditions,' in which she egged on the little ones to creep out of bed at crack of dawn 'and then to rampage in to cupboards, outhouses, &c., not accessible to children at other hours,' returning to bed without being caught by their parents. The salient difference between the Winkworths and the Brontës lies in the transition from a performed to a textual and privately 'published' world. No literature was generated by the Winkworth games. Though Catherine kept a journal from 1839 until 1843, it was a neat and unvarnished account of everyday proceedings in the household. The Brontë books by contrast are imaginatively spelt, madly punctuated and exotic.

A more anomalous feature of the Brontës' childhood play is its persistence into adult life. For Branwell, Charlotte, and Emily, the given world would never be enough. The collision of their imaginary worlds with the given reality would lead to Branwell's failures, addictions, and death, Emily's retreat and Charlotte's near-breakdown. Only when she wrote *Jane Eyre* could Charlotte bring the two worlds into reconciled alliance. Emily's diary papers show the seamlessness of the Gondal and quotidian Parsonage reality: 'the Gondals are discovering the interior of Gaaldine,' she writes at the age of sixteen, in her diary paper of 1834, continuing, 'Sally mosley is washing in the back kitchin' (Barker 1994, 221). In their mid-twenties, she and Anne were still playing the game of Gondal. On an expedition to York in 1845, Emily records that:

> though the weather was broken we enjoyed ourselves very much, except during a few hours at Bradford and during our excursions we were Ronald Macelgin, Henry Angora, Juliet Augusteena, Rosobelle Esraldan, Ella and Julia Egramont Catherine Navarre and Cordelia Fitzaphnold escaping from the Palaces of Instruction to join the Royalists who are hard driven at present by the victorious Republicans ... We intend sticking by the Rascals as long as they delight us, which I am glad to say they do at present. (Barker 1994, 451)

For Emily, the two young women are actor-writer-directors in a troupe of two, themselves their own audience, the world their theatre. They improvise story-lines and try out speeches for later transcription. Any role, male or female, can be adopted like a mask. Anne, the only sibling to abandon the thrill of the dream world in the face of practical and moral constraints, commented more bleakly, 'The Gondals in general are not in first-rate playing condition. Will they improve?' For her, Gondal's children were the playthings of childhood; for Emily, they were constant companions.

After Charlotte's death, Mrs Gaskell found manuscripts that seemed barely sane to her. When Charlotte took up a position as teacher at Miss Wooler's School at Roe Head in 1835, she was in a state of barely contained revolt. Emily was sent with her as pupil. Central to the Brontës' habits of composition – as for most writers – was the mind's freedom to wander the maze of imagination, without forcing or pressure. The psychologist Mihaly Csikszentmihalyi has described the conditions for creative 'flow' as an autotelic merging of action and awareness, an absence of distraction and self-consciousness, a forgetfulness of self, time, and surroundings (Csikszentmihalyi 1997, 110–23). When Charlotte and Emily left home for life in a community, their duties (regarded by Charlotte as menial) exiled them from all these conditions. Emily even had to share a bed with another pupil; always a light sleeper, but often blissfully awake in her Parsonage room at night, she was insomniac at Roe Head. She starved, literally and metaphorically. While all three sisters were painfully shy and self-conscious, Emily was withdrawn to an extreme degree and cut an odd figure, tall, lanky, strangely dressed (Chitham 1987, 85–9). She did not try to make friends. Cut off from Anne, she was barred out of their joint fantasy world of Gondal. 'Liberty was the breath of Emily's nostrils,' Charlotte recorded; 'without it, she perished … Every morning when she woke, the vision of home and the moors rushed on her, and darkened and saddened the day that lay before her … I felt in my heart she would die if she did not go home' ('Introduction,' E. Brontë 1995, 372).

For Charlotte, walled up at Roe Head as a teacher, the mundane round forced the Angrian narrative to the margins. When the repressed returned, it did so with a vengeance:

> Never shall I Charlotte Brontë forget what a voice of wild & wailing music Now came thrillingly to my mind's almost to my body's ear nor how distinctly I … sitting in the schoolroom at Roe-head … saw the Duke of Zamorna leaning against that obelisk … the fern waving at his feet his black horse turned loose grazing among the heather … the African sky quivering & shaking with stars expanded above all, I was quite gone I had really utterly forgot where I was and all the gloom & cheerlessness of my situation I felt myself breathing quick & short as I beheld … the Duke lifting up his sable crest …

as [music] was exciting him & quickening his ever rapid pulse 'Miss
Brontë what are you thinking about?' said a voice that dissipated all
the charm & Miss Lister thrust her little rough black head into my
face, 'Sic transit' &c (Barker 1994, 238–9)

The fact that this record was written in retrospect, on Charlotte's
return to Haworth for Christmas, indicates the power and heat of
the original experience. Zoned out of the normal world, Charlotte is
both hearing and seeing things: 'I was quite gone.' Zamorna, erotic,
heroic, and Byronic, makes her breathe short, physically aware of his
pulse, 'ever rapid,' answering and arousing hers. We sense her over-
breathing as she writes, for Zamorna is made of Charlotte's adolescent
desire. That was what he was for: to excite desire spiced with delicious
fear. At some level Charlotte recognized the fantasy as sexual. These
children of an Anglican minister were born not of the Victorian era
but of the Regency and of Romanticism. They were Byron's children.
This imagination had been nourished on the libertine, visionary and
intoxicated excesses of Romanticism. Yet simultaneously, Charlotte was
appalled by her own immoral imaginings, as at depravity. There existed
no language for female sexuality. *Jane Eyre* and *Villette* would articulate
such a language.

   She seems to have practised, at least in earlier life, automatic or
trance writing. In 1836, Charlotte recorded that, surrounded by people
'all wondering why I write with my eyes shut – staring, gasping, hang
their astonishment,' she retreated to inner space and shut her eyelids
like blinds, in the effort to render simultaneous imaginative experience and its transmission to the page: 'Stupidity the atmostphere
[sic], school-books the employment, asses the society, what in all this
is there to remind me of the divine, silent, unseen land of thought'
(Barker 1994, 255). The most authentic writing, to Charlotte, was the
most immediate; conception and expression should be simultaneous.
Privileging *ekstasis* above *techne*, she constructed inspiration as dictation from beyond. In trance writing, she literally shut her eyes to
the intrusions of her fellows, writing blind.[1] Trance writing ensured
fluency, which in turn engendered confidence. The manuscript of *Jane
Eyre* evidences this fluent confidence, as perhaps does the characteristic
sentence form: long sentences whose fundamental unit, attached para-
tactically, is a sequence of short main clauses strung together on semi-

---

[1]   She was, in any case, severely myopic, in an age when ophthalmology was
not highly advanced. Myopia blurs and distances the 'real' world.

colons. A favoured punctuation mark was the dash, a radically informal sign, equivalent to a breath.

At times the fantasy world threw Charlotte, all but literally. She records lying on her bed, wide awake in the dark, aware of her fellows fiddling with their curl papers. She tries to get up but cannot rise, 'as if some huge animal had flung itself across me' (Barker 1994, 256). 'I must get up I thought & I did so with a start. I have had enough of morbidly vivid realisations every advantage has its corresponding disadvantage.' The creature weighing on her body evokes Fuseli's Gothic oil painting, 'The Nightmare' of 1781/2, a Romantic and erotic image of female impotence before the subconscious mind. On a sleeping woman's chest perches a demonic incubus, a wild-eyed horse behind them. In the Romanticism Charlotte inherited, reverie and daydream were poetry's condition and source. They were also sources of psychic danger – a danger Charlotte is aware of here – the takeover of the paralysed will by predatory sexual compulsions. Conflict generates paranoia ('I heard them talking about me'). Charlotte's novels would explore the mind's terrors when the membrane between conscious and unconscious worlds is penetrated. We remember the 'avenging dream … a nameless experience' of *Villette* in which 'a cup was forced to my lips, black, strong, strange,' the bitter water of despair in a world of spectres and death's heads (C. Brontë 2000b, 159–60). These visitations are personified, attributed to agents outside the self. They are the rapacious converse of the creative imagination.

The visionary world was, for all four Brontës, a visual one. Germane to their creativity was the practice of the visual arts. Branwell may have been sent to the Royal Academy in 1835, though it is doubtful that he ever actually set foot in it (Barker 1994, 226–31). He practised as a portrait artist and was the only sibling to paint in oils (a male and elite medium). The fact that the heroine of Anne's *The Tenant of Wildfell Hall* is a professional painter is the measure of the novel's feminism. All four drew in 'black lead' pencil or pen and ink, painted in watercolour and sketched, sometimes working from engravings according to the 'copying' principle of their age (though Emily is known to have objected to copying literary models as detrimental to originality; her paintings and sketches are notably more free than those of her sisters). Charlotte's widower, Arthur Bell Nicholls, carefully preserved his wife's paintbox, in which were twenty-three cakes of paint in varying states of wear, porcelain mixing wells and palettes, tiny lead pencil, steel nib pen, and two hog-hair paint brushes, one made from a quill. Drawing and painting came as naturally as writing and, from the first, the two elder children would illustrate their writings. In *Jane Eyre*, Mr Rochester 'reads' Jane's soul through a series of visionary paintings, Romantic seascapes in the 'sublime' mode. Dismissing her technique as immature, he comments: 'These eyes in the Evening Star you must have seen in a dream ... and who taught you to paint wind?' (C. Brontë 2006, 148). It is clear that the pictures illustrate Jane's 'bright visions ... a tale that was never ended – a tale my imagination created, and narrated continuously' in the preceding chapter, linked there with women's rebellion (129–30).

Emily offers visual windows into the creativity of the Parsonage world. She left twenty-nine paintings and drawings, of which the most moving and beautiful are animal portraits, done when she returned from Brussels in 1842. The portrait of her ferocious labrador/mastiff crossbreed, Keeper, 'From Life,' shows her respect and affection for animal life (for her, a standard of integrity against which she judged human beings). It also shows her focused confidence with line and watercolour medium. On a pencilled outline, she works a base of colour, building the texture of Keeper's sandy coat and shadowy folds with minute brush strokes: we are aware of the creature's bulk, resting his fierce face on outstretched paws. The portrait captures the unique ease and fellowship Emily found in the company of animals.

During the sickness and deaths of her brother and sisters in 1848–49, Charlotte was engaged in writing her second published novel, *Shirley*. The central character memorialized Emily, 'as she might have been had she been placed in health and prosperity' (Barker 1994, 612). In the character of Shirley and her dog, Tartar, Charlotte sketched Emily reading, sitting on a low stool or on the rug before the fire, 'the tawny and lion-like bulk of Tartar ... stretched beside her, one hand on his head, the other holding a book.' The novel's insistence on Shirley's 'indolence' accords with the 'idleness' Emily acknowledged in herself and was always preparing to correct (a habit of creative musing which contrasts with her capacity for intense studiousness). Her poetry manuscripts, with doodles, smears, blots, and crossings-out, exemplify this state of mind (Plate 14, Chitham 1987, 160–1). As the moon rises, Shirley wakens from her trance-like reading, to a visionary ecstasy. Charlotte goes on to say that, had Shirley been a poet, she would have written out 'the story that has been narrated, the song that has been sung to her', and thus possess what she was enabled to create (C. Brontë 2000a, 387–8). The bereaved Charlotte smooths the edges of her intransigent sister, and overstresses the involuntary nature of Emily's inspiration. In fact, Emily was a technician who edited and reworked her poetry; she did not take her poetry at dictation. Charlotte's is an edited ideal, a mingling of fantasy and observation: the book, the fire, the fellowship of the animal lead to the ecstasy of creativity.

Emily's arresting pen and ink sketches on the diary papers of 1841 and 1845 are a miniature view of the private world of composition. She views herself writing from behind, in a little scene that seems to be going on before our eyes. Comparison with snapshots (a term coined in 1860) is not anachronistic: hers was the age of Daguerre's invention of the daguerreotype, fascinated by the sensational power of camera and chemical process to preserve not only an optical image but an actual trace of the field of vision. Photographers proclaimed the death of the painting (Davies 1998, 9–10, 114–16). Such authenticity is precisely the effect of the sketches in Emily's diary papers, rapidly improvised within the moment.

The 1841 paper shows Emily and Anne composing the diary paper at the kitchen table; it is a picture of artists within a creative environment. The scribbled sketches, untidy, improvisational, utterly confident, show masterly grasp of gesture and posture. Emily trusts her scrawl to come out right and, because of this trust, it does. Anne sits forward, elbows on the table, face propped on hands, in an attitude of eager response. Her dress has full, leg-of-mutton sleeves; her hair is up in a topknot. Emily, facing her sister, sits on a stool, in the act of writing the diary paper, hair knotted in a bun. On the table is the tin box in which the diary papers were kept to be fished out, revealing the hopes and events of a bygone moment. In the 1845 paper, Emily is alone in her bedroom, Anne working away as governess. The writer is viewed – again from behind – seated on her low stool in the right-hand corner, her portable rosewood desk on her knee, pen in hand (and it looks to be her left hand [Chitham 1987, 169; Davies 1988, 12–14]). Keeper lies at Emily's feet and Anne's spaniel, Flossy, and a cat snooze on the bed, under the window. This laptop desk and Emily's wooden stool, still visible at the Parsonage today, suggest the mobility of Emily's creative life, which could be conducted indoors or out. Tabitha Ratcliffe, sister of Martha Brown, the Brontë servant, once owned both desk and stool and insisted that they be kept together. 'Miss Emily always carried the stool into the garden or put it before the kitchen fire and then put the desk on her knee when she was about writing' (Alexander and Sellars 1995, 103). The possibility that Emily Brontë was left-handed has significant implications in terms of modern left-brain, right-brain theories of creativity. It is supported by the evidence of inverted spellings, awkward handwriting, musical ability and spatial dexterity, ideological reversal, as well as the mathematical exactitude of her narrative structuring in *Wuthering Heights* and her tendency to antithesis and chiasmus (Davies 1988, 12–14). Left-handedness often runs in families: the ambidextrous Branwell could write simultaneous but different texts using both hands.

Life-writing (both in the form of diary paper, journal, and letter) was essential to Brontë creativity. In *Wuthering Heights*, narrative polyphony creates distance, irony, and relativism, a coded world denying inter-pretative security. Despite this sophisticated narrative technique and intricate planning, dream and personal testament are as essential to its conception. On the window ledge by Cathy's box bed at the Heights, Lockwood finds graffiti: '*Catherine Earnshaw*, here and there varied to *Catherine Heathcliff*, and then again to *Catherine Linton* … the air swarmed with Catherines.' He riffles through Catherine's books, starting with a testament, whose fly leaf is inscribed 'Catherine Earn-shaw' and dated a quarter of a century back. Catherine has covered 'every morsel of blank' and every decent-sized margin with marginalia, some in the form of detached sentences, though 'other parts took the form of a regular diary, scrawled in an unformed, childish hand.' There's a wicked cartoon of Joseph, doubtless in the style of the scribble-art on Emily's diary papers. On one precious blank page, the snooper finds a fragment of diary:

> An Awful Sunday! … I wish my father were back again. Hindley is a detestable substitute – his conduct to Heathcliff is atrocious – H. and I are going to rebel – we took our initiatory step this morning. (18)

The exclamatory immediacy of Catherine's outpouring sets off the narrator's quest. Lockwood never learns, nor are we told, the full story. Emily and Anne's diary papers delighted them and excite us because of their relationship with time. They are designed as fragments, capturing the serendipitous moment within the vast continuum of unrecorded time. That moment, elusive and commonplace as it is, is also the crea-tive moment. And we first come upon Catherine Earnshaw not just as a narrator in a novel of many narrations, but as a writer of her own life and a budding cartoonist. Writing is agency, revenge, rebellion.

What of writing as themselves? Only three, laconic letters by Emily to people outside the family survive: in one she states that she rarely writes letters and does not propose to start now (Brontë, ed. Smith 1995, 319). But Charlotte, a voluminous letter writer, was a virtuoso of a form in which the nineteenth century was especially rich. When she married, the freedom and lack of discretion manifested in Charlotte's letters shocked her husband, who instructed her to tell Ellen Nussey to 'burn' (underlined three times) the current letter. 'Arthur says such letters as mine never ought to be kept – they are dangerous as lucifer matches – so be sure to follow a recommendation he has just given "fire them" – or "there will be no more"' (C. Brontë 1995, 1). Charlotte professes to find this amusing. Arthur couldn't mean it. After all, she'd said nothing 'rash.' He did of course mean it. In ink that has turned with time pale or medium brown, Charlotte had been writing her heart out to friends for a quarter of a century. We can follow the changes of her handwriting, from an early finely pointed penmanship, in a formal, well-spaced copperplate (1829–37), to a looser, more irregular hand, using thicker nibs and darker ink (1838–40) and a final small, flowing, even and regularly sloped hand, using a fine nib (1844–55) (C. Brontë 1995, 73). Yet, like her novels, these letters at once wear their hearts on their sleeves and clasp their secrets tight to the chest. The *cris de coeurs* she sent to Constantin Heger on returning from Belgium, written in French, carry a note of urgent need. This passion, however, is never shared with Charlotte's confidante, Ellen Nussey. The frank-seeming letters sent to Ellen were often cover-ups. Similarly, in *Villette*, whose M. Paul Emanuel is modelled on Heger, the narrator refuses the reader salient, indeed vital, information: what precipitated Lucy's breakdown? how did events fall out with M. Paul? Letters and novels expose the naked heart beneath a thick smokescreen. All Charlotte's writing is rashly self-expressive. The mode of expression in the letters offers clues to the novels' creativity:

> Monsieur, the poor do not need a great deal to live on – they ask only the crumbs of bread which fall from the rich men's table – but if they are refused these crumbs – they die of hunger
>
> (C. Brontë 1995, 379)

Voice is everything here: the panting, anguished human voice begging its 'master' for succour, as if he were her Maker, in a vein both biblical and personal. Lucy Snowe expresses a comparably psalmic hunger. The letters to M. Heger were chiefly written in French, as are portions of *The Professor* and *Villette*: a foreign language allowed their writer to construct herself in a more abandoned way than would English.

There is one difference, though, between the voice of letters and novels. Charlotte allowed the letters to go uncorrected: 'I don't want to reread this letter – I am sending it as I have written it,' aware that it might be said, 'she is raving' (C. Brontë 1995, 379–80). In fiction, however, Charlotte corrected and edited after the first outpouring. The status of a letter is midway between spoken and literary English. One of Charlotte's gifts to the novel form is to reintroduce into it the conversational immediacy and the full resonance of a woman's voice heard also in her letters.

In 1845–47, preparation of *Poems by Currer, Ellis and Acton Bell*, *Agnes Grey*, *Wuthering Heights*, *The Professor*, *Jane Eyre*, and *The Tenant of Wildfell Hall* revived the ambitious literary endeavours of childhood and again turned the Parsonage at Haworth into a force field of creativity – with the poignant difference that Branwell was excluded. Composition balanced individual privacy with corporate thought. The image of the sisters circling the table in the dining-room comes via Elizabeth Gaskell, who met Charlotte and became a close friend only after her sisters were dead:

> She went on with her work steadily. But it was dreary to write without any one to listen to the progress of her tale, – to find fault or to sympathise, – while pacing the length of the parlour in the evenings … Three sisters had done this, – then two, the other sister dropping off from the walk, – and now one was left desolate …
>   But she wrote on. (Gaskell 1997, 300)

Mrs Gaskell had learned this from a family servant, having heard when she retired at night the disquieting sound of Charlotte pacing the room below. Looking into the drawing-room, it is hard to imagine this whirling walk. The space is tiny. It suggests the closeness of these three minds, whose work not only expresses an individual vision but also a complex interaction of response and debate. Charlotte's work was not the less a product of this community of three writers when, tasting the bitter ashes of celebrity, she circled in their footsteps alone.

Now

Mr Brontë told Elizabeth Gaskell that, when his children were small, he stood them one by one behind a mask, to elicit their true opinions. This stroke of brilliance, suggested perhaps by ancient Greek drama, released the characteristic inner voice of each. The face disappeared: the voice remained.

I have been asked, in this coda, to speak of my own debt to the

Brontës: I can only compare it with the release of voice. In *Wuthering Heights*, Heathcliff grieves for Cathy: 'I *cannot* live without my life! I *cannot* live without my soul!' (E. Brontë 1995, 167). I find that, in my historical novel *Impassioned Clay*, I have unconsciously echoed Heathcliff's cry in the words of seventeenth-century renegade Quaker and ecstatic preacher Hannah Jones. She reacts to the Quakers' attempt to suppress her in this dream:

> As James [Nayler] prevailed, so I lost ground, & my voice was lost, as if the wind had swept it away over the barren.
> But I said, 'I cannot live without my Voice'…
> But still, though I was only a pool of water, scooped in his palm, I could not surrender; & I cried out with a loud voice, 'I must speak!'
> (Davies 1999, 180)

Catherine Earnshaw exclaims to Nelly that 'I've dreamt in my life dreams that have stayed with me ever after, and changed my ideas; they've gone through and through me, like wine through water, and altered the colour of my mind' (79). Reading can induce just such a state of reverie and communion, a dreaming awake in which the boundaries between reader and writer seem to dissolve, until they are one creative mind. *Wuthering Heights* must have been floating in my mind, without conscious awareness: the telling of a life-changing dream; allusion to 'the barren' (the northern word for 'moor'); the variation on Heathcliff's *cri de coeur*. While Heathcliff asserts a needy pathology of identification with Catherine, Hannah refuses identification with her friend, at absolute personal cost, to speak out her own truth. Women writers are indebted to the Brontës for the liberation of their voices.

Works Cited

Alexander, Christine, and Sellars, Jane, 1995. *The Art of the Brontës*. Cambridge: University of Cambridge Press.

Barker, Juliet, 1994. *The Brontës*. London: Weidenfeld & Nicolson.

Brontë, Anne, 1996. *The Tenant of Wildfell Hall*, ed. Stevie Davies. London: Penguin.

Brontë, Charlotte, 1995. *The Letters of Charlotte Brontë*, Volume One, 1829–1847, ed. Margaret Smith. Oxford: Clarendon Press.

Brontë, Charlotte, 1996. *Juvenilia 1829–1835*, ed. Juliet Barker. London: Penguin.

Brontë, Charlotte, 2000a. *Shirley*, ed. Herbert Rosengarten and Margaret Smith. Oxford: Oxford University Press.

Brontë, Charlotte, 2000b. *Villette*, ed. Herbert Rosengarten and Margaret Smith. Oxford: Oxford World's Classics.

Brontë, Charlotte, 2006. *Jane Eyre*, ed. Stevie Davies. London: Penguin.

Brontë, Charlotte and Emily, 1996. *The Belgian Essays: A Critical Edition*, trans. and ed. Sue Lonoff. New Haven & London: Yale University Press.

Brontë, Emily, 1995. *Wuthering Heights*, ed. Ian Jack and Patsy Stoneman. Oxford & New York: Oxford University Press.

Chitham, Edward, 1987. *A Life of Emily Brontë*. Oxford: Basil Blackwell.

Csikszentmihalyi, Mihaly, 1997. *Creativity: Flow and the Psychology of Discovery and Invention*. London: HarperPerennial.

Davies, Stevie, 1988. *Emily Brontë*. New York & London: Harvester Wheatsheaf.

Davies, Stevie, 1994. *Emily Brontë: Heretic*. London: The Women's Press.

Davies, Stevie, 1998. *Emily Brontë*. Plymouth: Northcote House with the British Council.

Davies, Stevie, 1999. *Impassioned Clay*. London: The Women's Press.

Gaskell, Elizabeth, 1997. *The Life of Charlotte Brontë*, ed. Elisabeth Jay. London: Penguin.

Winkworth, S. and C., 1908. *Memorials of Two Sisters: Susanna and Catherine Winkworth*, ed. M. J. Shaen. London: Longmans, Green.

Literary Festivals: Hay-on-Wye

GRAEME HARPER interviews PETER FLORENCE

GH: How did you come to start the Hay Festival? Inspiration or aspiration – or was it frustration?

PF: I had toured the world with a one-man show for the British Council and played a lot of festivals and loved the buzz. I also played Cheltenham and liked it, but wanted to adapt it a little to where I lived.

GH: Hay – the place – is a fairly distinctive 'environment,' isn't it?

PF: Hay is a byword for laid-back hedonistic liberalism. It's traditionally been a book-lovers' paradise, but locals know it as a farming market town. For fifty weeks a year it deals in livestock, for the two weeks of the festivals it trades stories and ideas.

GH: And the Hay 'experience'?

PF: A few years ago the *New York Times* described the festival as a cross between university finals and a country wedding. I like that. It was born really of my dissatisfaction with both academia and show-business. We've made a talky party, I guess.

GH: Hay has a political element to it. Some of that can be quite directly related to the contemporary events and debates held here; some of it seems to generally attach itself to the Hay Festival being about ideas.

PF: The festival is committedly progressive, and there's a direct link between the open-mindedness that 'gets' literature, and a receptiveness to good wine, smart comedians, and political adventure. Writers are relentlessly exacting and hostile to any prevailing political orthodoxy. The Labour government's relationship with the leftish literary establishment is one of extreme ambivalence.

GH: Writers come to the festival, they launch their books, talk about their books. Other things are going on, non-writerly things, and the whole atmosphere is pretty vibrant and interpersonal! Do you think this shows anything about how writers view their work, or even how they might view their readers and audiences?

PF: A literary festival is like the out-takes and commentary DVD in a boxed set. What we do is make things more accessible and – yes – FUN – our highest accolade. Reading's a private pleasure, and it engages the intellect more than any other art form. We've tried to make literary criticism part of the entertainment industry, by using it to enrich people's love of books, and setting it in a context of a party rather than a classroom. And for readers – there's nothing more exciting than discovering a new voice or story. Writers are great companions. We find writers are hugely articulate thinkers whose books qualify them as valuable commentators on life, love, death, and the whole shebang. They can be paranoid, misanthropic, envious, generous, inspiring, and thrilling just like everyone else – but they can talk about it.

GH: You also write yourself?

PF: There's a great Peter Cook & Barry Fatoni cartoon which I was given: Two guys are standing in what is obviously the Groucho Club or similar. One says to the other 'I'm writing a novel.' The other says 'Neither am I …'

GH: Hay seems to be focused on the 'now,' not just in the books talked about but its interest in the use of new technologies and current debates. Any comment?

PF: Hay assumes a basic literacy I suppose. We aim to be the best of the best, not a generalist's introduction. Flipside, according to George Steiner – and I think he's bang on the money – festivals have to do three things: celebrate the greatest contemporary practitioners, reclaim reputations that have fallen victim to fashions, and identify and nurture the most promising voices of the future. I'm more focused on number three than number two. Others might not be.

GH: Can you say a little more about the 'other' Hay Festivals, and about how the idea to travel 'Hay' emerged?

PF: We go where there are great writers, good food, and sunshine – for a change! We went to Colombia because we couldn't get Garcia Marquez to come here. Spain spun out of our adventures in Hispanic literature. We're moving now to Nairobi, Beirut, and Bangladesh to engage more fully with the African, Arab, and Muslim worlds, which seem to me now to be the most compelling areas to explore. Writers open cultures far more vividly than journalists and TV.

GH: With that worldwide spread, do you ever imagine the major 'Hay' not being in Hay in some respect?

PF: We'd never design what Hay has become now. It's an insane nine-ring circus. The eccentricity and intellectual promiscuity is very British; the gathering is very Welsh; the programming reflects Britain's unique global location being extra-European, transatlantic, and part of a Common Wealth of Anglophone traditions.

GH: The term 'cultural entrepreneur' is sometimes attached to you –

PF: – on bad days you feel like a wine-waiter or a pimp, on good days you see people change their minds. I'll go with whatever label people like. The job feels most like parenting.

GH: The basics: what's the timetable for getting a festival together (in its original Hay guise, or in any of its international guises), and what are the key milestones?

PF: It never stops. Every conversation, book, radio bulletin or news-paper stimulates ideas. We now have one festival every two months somewhere in the world. It's sometimes hard to remember what's in our heads, what's on the grid, in the brochure, or about to kick-off. The interesting thing is how an invitation to Wales in 1995 can sometimes be realized as a lecture in Granada thirteen years later.

GH: Do things change much along the way? And how often do things go wrong?

PF: Hay, Mantova, Parati, and Deia grew organically. We learned how to do things more efficiently for Colombia and Spain. Things go horribly wrong every festival and you never know what they'll be. We have a wrap document for each festival to identify stuff to correct or improve. Everyone feeds into it.

GH: Finally, an interviewer cliché! Some of the most significant occurrences over the years of the festival?

PF: Meeting Seamus Heaney – hearing Wangari Maathai – dancing to Ian Dury as he sang 'From The Gardens of Bombay all the way to Lovely Hay, Hit Me With Your Rhythm Stick.' I've loved it all, but you also have to have a sense of perspective. We're not doing anything vitally important. It's not like we're teachers or doctors or soldiers where you save or make people's lives. If it all goes wrong the worst that'll happen is some people will be bored. The best that can happen though is liberation, enlightenment, and adventure – so it's worth trying to get it right.

Composing Paradise Lost: Blindness and the Feminine

PETER C. HERMAN

HOW DID THE MATERIAL CIRCUMSTANCES of Milton's situation shape *Paradise Lost*? The following essay argues that two problems were reworked into opportunities in the composition of the poem. His blindness forced Milton to explore the use of multiple voices and multiple narrators, and his subsequent reliance on his daughters led him to reassess the feminine aspect of creativity.

The early lives of Milton – those by John Aubrey (1681), an anonymous, undated life now ascribed to Cyriack Skinner, Anthony à Wood (1691), Edward Phillips (1694), John Toland (1698), and Jonathan Richardson (1734) – contain much information on how Milton went about the task (Darbishire 1932). John Aubrey said it took Milton about '4 or 5 yeares' to create *Paradise Lost*, and that 'He began about 2 yeares before the K. [King] came-in, and finished about 3 yeares after the K's Restauracon [Restoration]' (Darbishire 1932, 13), that is, between 1658 and 1663. Four more years would elapse between finishing the poem and the publication of the first edition as a ten-book poem in 1667. A second edition, in which Milton increased the number of books to twelve, added the explanatory notes, and revised some lines, appeared in 1671.

It had taken years of mulling over this project before its form and content became clear to the author. From the start of his poetic career, Milton signalled that his ambitions exceeded those of any other English poet. In Elegy 6, a verse-letter to his friend Charles Diodati, Milton declared his intention to become a poet who 'sings of wars, of Heaven ruled by a Jove no longer a boy, of dutiful heroes, of commanders who are demigods' (55–6).[1] He intended to become an epic poet, in other words, when for at least a century poetic theorists had agreed with the ancients that the epic was the highest form of poetry. 'All concurreth to the maintaining the heroical, which is not only a kind, but the best and most accomplished kind of poetry. For as the image of each action

---

[1]   All references to Milton's poetry and prose are to the Riverside edition (1998), except where noted.

stirreth and instructeth the mind, so the lofty image of such worthies most inflameth the mind with desire to be worthy, and informs with counsel how to be worthy,' writes Sir Philip Sidney in *An Apology for Poetry* (Sidney 2001, 92). In 1677, John Dryden concurs: 'Heroique Poetry ... has ever been esteem'd, and ever will be, the greatest work of human Nature' (Milton 1998, 334).

Yet Milton's ambitions go one step further. In Elegy 6 he tells Diodati that he is presently writing 'On the Morning of Christ's Nativity.' In this poem the speaker urges his muse to 'joyn thy voice unto the Angel Quire, / From out his secret Altar toucht with hallow'd fire' (27–8). The allusion to Isaiah 6:5–7, in which an angel touches the prophet's lips with a burning coal to purify them, announces Milton's ambition to become England's divinely inspired poet-prophet. None of the previous century's poets had made such a claim, not even Edmund Spenser, the 'sage and serious Poet' as Milton calls him (1006), who was merely ambitious to become England's epic poet (Helgerson 1983, 55–100), nor Sidney, praising poetry as superior to history and philosophy for inspiring virtuous action but explicitly distancing himself from Plato, who in the *Ion* 'attributeth unto poesy more than myself do, namely, to be a very inspiring of a divine force, far above man's wit' (Sidney 2001, 107). The claims for divine inspiration Milton made in 'The Nativity Ode,' anticipating those of *Paradise Lost*, go beyond these boundaries.

Yet Milton's early plans were not fulfilled, or at least, not in the short term. In the biographical digression in *The Reason of Church Government* (1642), Milton testified to his desire to write a great poetic work (whether epic or tragedy he is not sure), one that would combine 'the office of a pulpit, to inbreed and cherish in a great people the seeds of vertu, and publick civility.' But 'time servs not now': the threat of prelacy is too great, and the crises engulfing England make it 'folly to commit any thing elaborately compos'd to the careless and interrupted listening of these tumultuous times.' Therefore he has put aside the soaring fancies of poetry to embrace 'the cool element of prose' (922–3). Even so, the project of writing an epic was never far from Milton's mind. Aubrey notes that Edward Phillips (Milton's nephew) recalled reading 'about 6 verses of Satan's exclamation to the Sun, wch Mr E. Ph. Remembers, about 15 or 16 yeares before ever his Poëm was thought of [that is, circa 1642], wch verses were intended for the Beginning of a Tragoedie wch he had designed, but was diverted from it by other business' (Darbishire 1932, 13). [2] In 1658, with the experiment

---

[2]   Milton had jotted down plans for possible tragedies in a commonplace book,

in non-monarchical rule collapsing, Milton finally returned to his long-delayed epic project: 'this Subject for Heroic Song / Pleas'd me long choosing, and beginning late' (*PL* 9. 25–6).

Changing jobs, family circumstances, and political exigencies meant that Milton lived in a variety of residences over the decades of planning, writing, and revising *Paradise Lost*. His mode of working, however, does not seem to have varied. The anonymous life of Milton says that the morning, immediately after waking, was Milton's best time for poetic creativity. He

> rendred his Studies and various Works more easy & pleasant by allotting them thir several portions of the day. Of these the time friendly to the Muses fell to his Poetry; And hee waking early (as is the use of temperate men) had commonly a good Stock of Verses ready against his Amanuensis came; which if it happened to bee later than ordinary, hee would complain, Saying *hee wanted to bee milkd*. (Darbishire 1932, 33)

This description comes back in Milton's assertion in the proem to Book 9 that the Muse, his 'Celestial Patroness,' deigns 'Her nightly visitation unimplor'd, / And dictates to me slumbring, or inspires / Easie my unpremeditated Verse' (9. 21–4). Edward Phillips gives a similar account: 'for some years, as I went from time to time, to Visit him, [there was] a Parcel of Ten, Twenty, or Thirty Verses at a Time, which being written by whatever hand came next, might possibly want Correction as to the Orthography and Pointing' (Darbishire 1932, 73). A number of such amanuenses were used: daughters, nephews, and other family members, and scholars wanting to work with a famously learned man. Decades later, Jonathan Richardson is still engaged with this process of inspiration and release. At

> times flow'd *Easy his Unpremeditated Verse*, with a certain *Impetus* and *Aestro*, as Himself seem'd to Believe. Then, at what Hour soever, he rung for his Daughter to secure what Came. I have been also told he would Dictate many, perhaps 40 Lines as it were in a Breath, and then reduce them to half the Number. (Darbishire 1932, 291)

now known as the Trinity Manuscript (Milton 1953–82, viii. 539–85). The final form of Satan's address to the sun is in *Paradise Lost* 4. 32–113.

Plate 4: Arthur Dixon, 'Blind Milton Dictating his Immortal Poem,' in *Newnes' Pictorial Book of Knowledge*.

Sometimes this dictation took place in bed; sometimes, Richardson says, Milton instead 'Sat leaning Backward Obliquely in an Easy Chair, with his Leg flung over the Elbow of it' (Darbishire 1932, 291).

From the late eighteenth to the early twentieth century, a variety of artists painted Milton's dictation of *Paradise Lost*. Abandoning the details of Milton's fractious domestic and political life, they contribute to the dominant narrative of a calm work environment shaping a transcendent poem. These artists imagined, as did Samuel Taylor Coleridge, that 'finding it impossible to realize his own aspirations, either in religion, or politics, or society, [Milton] gave up his heart to the living spirit and light within him, and avenged himself on the world by enriching it with this record of his own transcendent ideal' (Coleridge 1950, 97). They ignore all male amanuenses, preferring instead to depict Milton dictating his epic to his daughters, who are usually shown attending carefully to the words of their father. For instance, Arthur Dixon's consciously charming early-twentieth-century lithograph sets the scene in Milton's cottage in Chalfont St Giles (incidentally, the only one of Milton's many residences still standing). Dixon portrays a little domestic and rural paradise (Plate 4).

In the picture, the light streaming through the window brings together Milton's habit of sunning himself in good weather (though, in fact, the early lives say he sat outside) with his address to the Muse at the beginning of Book 3:

> Hail holy Light, ofspring of Heav'n first born,
> Or of th'Eternal Coeternal beam
> May I express thee unblam'd? since God is light,
> And never but in approached light
> Dwelt from Eternitie, dwelt then in thee,
> Bright effluence of bright essence increate. (*PL* 3. 1–6)

The same details reoccur in paintings for adults, such as Soma Orlai Petrics's 1862 'Milton dictating Paradise Lost to his Daughters.' In this painting, Milton, in the centre of the canvas, sits in a chair with one leg resting on a stool. He is next to a window opening onto a lovely pastoral scene and surrounded by all three daughters, one of whom takes dictation. Again, the rural scene in the window suggests Chalfont St Giles, not London. All three of Milton's daughters are shown dutifully attending to their father's words (the one sitting on the left gazes at her father with rapt devotion). This image reproduces the reverence for masculine authority that many – mistakenly – have thought *Paradise*

Lost epitomizes; Woolf, for instance, called Milton the last of the masculinists (Woolf 1979; Gilbert 1978; Nyquist 1987). Such scenes of domestic serenity, also featured by artists such as Eugene Delacroix and George Romney, show Milton as a timeless poet rising above the dust and heat of politics (Herman 2006, 1–24).[3]

The curators of the only place remaining where Milton worked on his poem, the cottage in Chalfont St Giles, contribute to this narrative by seeking to replicate the domestic serenity supposedly enveloping the post-Restoration Milton. For instance, Milton's earliest biographer, John Aubrey, noted that he always had a garden where he lived (Darbishire 1932, 6), and every effort has been made to recall the description of Eden as filled with 'Flours worthy of Paradise which not nice Art / In Beds and curious Knots, But Nature boon / Powrd forth profuse' (4. 241–2). Visitors to Milton's garden are treated to a splendid display of brilliant flowers.

Such images from the nineteenth century onwards, of a blind Milton creating *Paradise Lost* in pastoral splendour, aided by his loving and obedient daughters, are highly selective about the actual conditions. The political atmosphere was anything but serene. As the experiment in non-monarchic rule began to fail, Milton's disillusionment grew. At the Restoration, Milton was forced underground. As Edward Phillips puts it, '[h]is next removal was, by the advice of those that wisht him sell, and had a concern for his preservation, into a place of retirement and abscondence' (Darbishire 1932, 74). Even though Parliament (after much debate) did not exclude him from the Act of Oblivion, Milton was briefly imprisoned, and after his release remained under suspicion.

Nor did his domestic life provide a refuge from the stress of disease, disaster, and political turmoil. Around February 1652 Milton lost the last of his eyesight. Mary Powell, Milton's first wife, died in May (probably from childbirth complications) and their son, John, died a month later, leaving Milton to care for their three daughters. In 1656, Milton married Katherine Woodcock, and a year later, they also had a daughter; both were dead within two years. Independence and confidence in domestic and working spaces come, for the blind, by being in familiar rooms and gardens. Yet the family moved extraordinarily often, as Milton was employed as Latin secretary by the Republic's Council

---

[3]   An exception to this is Henry Fuseli's uncanny 'Milton Dictating to his Daughters' (1794), where Milton huddles to the side in gloom, blind eyes cast up, while a ray of light touches his daughter standing, centre picture, at a writing desk.

of State and moved closer to his office work – evicted when Parliament began to control the accommodation it possessed – moved again into hiding at the Restoration – and again into more long-term private housing – and again at his third marriage – and again, when plague threatened. [4] All told, as Richardson says, Milton can have been far from serene while composing his epic:

> Disappointment on the Change of the Times, and from his Own Private Losses, and probably Cares for Subsistence, and for his Family; he was in Perpetual Terror of being Assassinated, though he had Escap'd the Talons of the Law, he knew he had Made Himself Enemies in Abundance. He was So Dejected he would lie Awake whole Nights. (Darbishire 1932, 275–6)

Romantic readers such as Shelley and Blake put forward a much more complex view of Milton, one that took into account the disturbing political aspects of *Paradise Lost* (Newlyn 1993). Some artists reflected this in a different fantasy of Milton's creative environment. Mihaly Munkacsy's 1878 painting of Milton dictating *Paradise Lost* to his daughters highlights what Dixon and the others repress (Plate 5). Milton here has a furrowed brow, a thin, mean face, and a fierce expression; he is surrounded by daughters (who clearly want to be anywhere but there). Far from reverence, their expressions bear out Phillips's opinion that reading books in Latin, Greek, Italian, and French out to Milton 'without understanding one word [… themselves was] a Tryal of Patience, almost beyond endurance' (Darbishire 1932, 77).

How then, in the midst of this political and domestic calamity, did Milton compose his long-delayed epic? Contrary to tradition, it was not by transcending his problems. In the proem to Book 3, Milton accepts blindness as the price for the divine gift of prophecy. He does not forget

---

[4]   At the end of 1651, Milton moved from Whitehall to 'a pretty Gardenhouse in Petty-France (York Street) in Westminster, next door to the Lord Scudamore's, and opening into St. James Park' (Darbishire 1932, 71), where he stayed until the Restoration, when he hid in a friend's house in Bartholomew Close. After he re-emerged, his friends arranged for temporary housing in Holborn, near the Red Lion Inn, where he stayed for a short time until a more suitable place was found on Jewin Street. The Miltons did not stay there long. Soon after his marriage to Elizabeth Minshull, Milton moved the family 'to a House in the *Artillery*-walk leading to *Bunhill Fields*' (Darbishire 1932, 75), which would be their London residence for the remainder of his life. For the summer and autumn of 1665, however, the Milton family lived at Chalfont St Giles, to escape the plague.

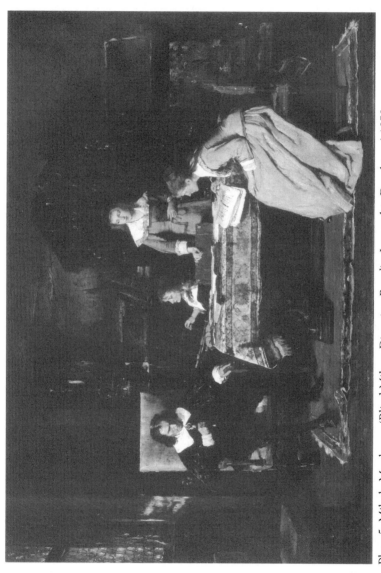

Plate 5: Mihaly Munkacsy, 'Blind Milton Dictating *Paradise Lost* to his Daughters,' 1878.

'Those other two equal'd with me in Fate, / So were I equal'd with them in renown, / Blind *Thamyris* and blind *Maeonides* / And *Tiresias* and *Phineus* Prophets old' (3. 32–6). Like them, his physical blindness signifies inner illumination: 'So much the rather thou Celestial light / Shine inward, and the mind through all her powers / Irradiate, there plant eyes, all mist from thence / Purge and disperse, that I may see and tell / Of things invisible to mortal sight' (3. 51–5). While Milton sees blindness as the precondition of writing *Paradise Lost*, he also registers a metaphysical danger, signalled by his choice of peers. Three out of the four of these prophets lost their sight as punishment for either their presumptuousness in challenging the gods or, in the case of Tiresias, for acquiring forbidden knowledge (Maeonides, that is Homer, is the exception: Milton 1998, 417, n. 20). Milton repeatedly refers in *Paradise Lost* to the transgressive potential of revealing, as Raphael puts it, 'The secrets of another world, perhaps / Not lawful to reveal' (5. 569–70). When he finishes expanding on the account in Genesis 1 of Creation, Raphael tells Adam that 'Heav'n is for thee too high / To know what passes there; be lowlie wise' (8. 172–3). Blindness creates opportunity, but also risk.

Then there is the social price Milton pays to enter the company of sightless prophets. Though he may wander by the imaginary Muse's haunts, 'Smit with the love of sacred Song' (3. 29), there is the agonizing social isolation brought on by blindness:

> ever-during dark
> Surrounds me, from the cheerful wayes of men
> Cut off, and for the Book of knowledge fair
> Presented with a Universal blanc
> Of Natures works to mee expung'd and ras'd,
> And wisdome at one entrance quite shut out. (3. 45–50)

Such unsought solitude has a political dimension: 'fall'n on evil dayes / … and evil tongues; / In darkness, and with dangers compast round, / And solitude' (7. 25–8). Nor will this epic teach a nation, since he expects that its 'fit' audience will be few (in contrast to his earlier hope of using verse to teach a nation about morality).

Milton's blindness also shapes the creative environment of *Paradise Lost* in the area of voice. For the blind Milton, hearing replaced eyesight as the prime means of receiving the world. Richardson recounts a story about how Milton, hearing a 'A Lady Sing Finely,' said '*This Lady is Handsom*'; 'His Ears Now were Eyes to Him' (Darbishire 1932, 204).

When Milton first announced his intention to become England's poet-prophet in 'The Nativity Ode,' he used a pun that gestured toward the materiality of poetic composition: 'joyn thy voice unto the Angel Quire' (27). The term 'Quire' brings together three contemporary references: a vocal 'choir,' a term signifying both a small book or pamphlet (especially one of four sheets of parchment or paper folded in two so as to form eight leaves), and a short poem or treatise which could be contained in such a book. The poem thus incorporates the means of its production – the conventional image of a poet in the heat of inspiration scribbling away on quires of paper. In *Paradise Lost*, however, composition cannot be imaged in terms of a concrete act of writing. Milton relies on *voice* to create his poem. He recites the lines in his head, and after the amanuenses scribble away on their own 'quires' of paper, they recite those lines back to Milton, who then orally edits them. The process of creation thus takes place in the ear, not the hand or the eye. Where the materiality of poetic composition is the central conceit of 'The Nativity Ode,' voice is the central vehicle for *Paradise Lost*.[5]

The epic begins with Milton asking the Muse to tell him 'what cause / Mov'd our Grand Parents in that happy State, / Favour'd of Heav'n so highly, to fall off / From thir Creator and transgress his Will' (1. 28–31). The Muse immediately *answers*, and the rest of the poem (excluding the proems in Books 3, 7, and 9, spoken by Milton) is in her voice. Later editions follow the first by printing these opening lines without quotation marks. However, adding them underscores how they show *two* voices in dialogue, without any intervening descriptions:

> 'Who first seduc'd them to that foul revolt?'
> 'Th'infernal Serpent; he it was, whose guile
> Stird up with Envy and Revenge, deceiv'd
> The Mother of Mankind.' (1. 33–6)

Within the Muse's speech that follows on, we have reported speeches by the other characters: Adam, Eve, God, Satan, Beelzebub, Abdiel, and so on. The passages that seem to emanate from a neutral omniscient narrator originate, in fact, from the voice of the Muse. She is neither omniscient (she is not sure whether the earth's axis shifted or the sun moved to a different position; 'Some say' either possibility

---

[5]   This section draws generally on Herman 2006 and the treatment of voice in Sauer 1996.

[10. 668, 671]) nor neutral (she introduces Belial's speech in the Great Consult by telling us that he 'could make the worse appear / The better reason' [2. 113–14] even though Belial's main point, the omniscience of God, is one she also uses).[6] Within this giant recitation by the Muse come further recitations within recitations. Thus in Book 3 God reports to the Angels that He has exalted the Son and gives his account of the present, past and future; Eve tells Adam the story of her beginnings (4. 440–92); the Creation is placed within Raphael's long discourse to Adam (Book 7), as is the War in Heaven (Book 6); and Adam fills in the gaps in Raphael's knowledge when he invites the angel 'to hear mee relate / My Storie' (8. 204–5). In the final two books, Michael follows God's command to 'reveale / To *Adam* what shall come in future dayes' (11. 113–14).

This models the process of composition: repeated repetition of material, through recitation from memory, reading back from dictation, and oral editing. However, it also gives a new emphasis to how the various speakers in *Paradise Lost* give differing interpretations or even differing versions of the most fundamental events. There are two sorts: those related by voices that either literary tradition or theology say should be read as trustworthy, and those related by lesser protagonists, who cannot claim omniscience.

Paradise Lost begins with Milton assuming that the Muse will give him the transcendent truth. Heaven, he claims at the poem's start, 'hides nothing from thy view, / Nor the deep Tract of Hell' (1. 27–8). The proem to Book 3 begins by conflating the Muse with God: 'Hail holy Light, ofspring of Heav'n first-born' (3. 1). The reader thus has every expectation that the Muse will tell us what exactly happened with no ambiguity. But, instead of uncontestable facts, Milton's *Paradise Lost* delivers the reader into a world where there is no Truth. Here, instead, are many truths, where different speakers give significantly varying, even contradictory, versions of the poem's key events – including the Fall, the Exaltation of the Son, Satan's rebellion – with no means provided for the reader of deciding between them. The small number of critics willing to register such contradictions have traced them back to a number of causes. There are theological explanations,

---

6 Belial argues against continuing the fight because God knows and sees everything: 'for what can force or guile / With him, or who deceive his mind, whose eye / Views all things at one view?' (2. 188–90); the Muse will make almost the same point later on: 'what can scape the Eye / Of God All-seeing, or deceave his Heart / Omniscient' (10. 5–7).

such as how to reconcile the demands of a self-consistent fiction with the demands made by an absolutely true scripture (Danielson 1982). There are differences in the source accounts, such as the two accounts of creation given in Genesis. There are changes to Milton's opinions over the lengthy period the poem took to compose (Lewalski 2003). My account gives a material reason for how these differences are registered: a multi-vocal epic that embodies the discursive mechanisms used to compose it.

When Milton asks the Muse who caused the Fall she replies that it is Satan's fault, 'Th'infernal Serpent; he it was' (1. 34). Yet when God asks the same question ('whose fault?' 3. 96) he gives a very different answer, 'Whose but his own? ingrate' (3. 97). Yet God says Adam 'falls deceiv'd' by Satan (3. 130), while the Muse seems to take up God's earlier position when she says that Adam fell, 'not deceav'd' by Satan 'But fondly overcome with Femal charm' (9. 998–9). The Muse and God, it seems, can agree on what happened but not on why, even in their own minds. Dividing the narrator off from the Muse and from God emphasizes this is a dialogue, with different voices. It makes for that seeming oxymoron, a flexible epic.

These divergences are as frequent (though perhaps less surprising) among the creations of God. For instance, the Muse and Raphael give differing versions of when the Exaltation of the Son occurred, and why Satan rebelled in the first place. In the Muse's telling, God summons the Angels after Satan leaves Hell and is flying 'Directly towards the new created World' (3. 89). Because the Son offers himself to redeem humankind, God rewards him:

> Therefore thy humiliation shall exact
> With thee thy Manhood also this Throne;
> Here shalt thou sit incarnate, here shalt Reign
> Anointed universal King. (3. 312–15)

Raphael, however, locates the Elevation of the Son in a different time and for a different reason. In his telling, the Elevation takes place *before* the world was created: 'As yet this world was not, and *Chaos* wilde / Reigned where these Heav'ns now rowl, where Earth now rests' (5. 577–8). Without any apparent cause, God summons the Angels and announces a change in Heaven's political structure:

> Hear all ye Angels, Progenie of Light,
> Thrones, Dominations, Princedoms, Vertues, Powers,

> Hear my Decree, which unrevok't shall stand.
> This day I have begot whom I declare
> My onely Son, and on this holy Hill
> Him have anointed, whom ye now behold
> At my right hand; your Head I him appoint. (5. 600–6)

According to the Muse, the Angels are universally delighted with this change: 'Heav'n rung / With Jubilee, and loud Hosannas filld / Th'eternal Regions' (3. 347–9). According to Raphael, the reaction was more qualified: 'So spake th'Omnipotent, and with his words / All seemd well plead's, all seem'd, but were not all' (5. 616–17).

This divergence leads to the differing views on why Satan rebelled. According to the Muse, when she speaks in her own voice, 'Pride / Had cast him out from Heav'n, with all his Host' (1. 36–7). However, in Raphael's conversation with Adam, God's sudden alteration of Heaven's political structure sparks Satan's rebellion. Turning to his 'Companion dear' (probably Beelzebub), Satan asks:

> remembrest what Decree
> Of yesterday, so late hath past the lips
> Of Heav'ns Almightie …
> New Laws thou seest impos'd;
> New Laws from him who reigns, new minds may raise
> In us who serve, new Counsels. (5. 673–81)

These differences are never commented on, by authorial persona, Muse, God, or any of the lesser creatures who listen and tell. Only the reader's memory of the voice – 'surely he said this, not that' – is left as an unsettling echo. Milton's creative environment – one of memorial recitation, dictation, and oral revision – provides a material reason why political and theological uncertainties can be figured as voices which revise earlier accounts.

The influence of the domestic creative environment on *Paradise Lost* turns out to be just as strong, in another way. Milton's relations with his daughters were far from happy. 'Nowhere in his writings or reported statements does he refer to them with love or tenderness' (Lewalski 2003, 508). During the probate hearings on Milton's will (an oral one, of course), his last maidservant describes a Lear-like family dynamic (Lewalski 2003, 409). Asked about his daughter Mary's response to Milton's intention to remarry,

> The said Mary replyed to the said Maidservant that that was noe News to heare of his wedding but if shee could heare of his death

that was something – and [Milton] further told this Respondent that
all his said Children did combine together and counsel his Maidservant to cheat him the decedent in hir Markettings, and that his
said children had made away some of his bookes and would have
solde the rest of his bookes to the Dunghill women

(quoted in Lewalski 2003, 409)

One might expect this poisonous atmosphere to infect Milton's treatment of gender in *Paradise Lost*, just as the political uncertainty did.
Far from it.

Artistic representations of Milton dictating his epic focus on his
daughters as his amanuenses, not on the many male hands that aided
him. In one sense though this is just, for Milton seems to have conceived
of writing the epic as a feminine act. He describes his readiness to
unburden himself of the verses in his head 'as Saying *hee wanted to
bee milkd*' (Darbishire 1932, 33), emphasizing passivity and femininity.
As Katharine Eisaman Maus argues, the period's frequent use of womb
imagery for creativity combined fear and praise (Maus 1995, 196).
It is the counterpart to the penis/pen pun. In *Astrophil and Stella*, for
instance, the Muse of the first sonnet impregnates the sonneteer but
also stops the birth, abuses him, and looks on sardonically as he beats
himself up for being unable to write feeling. Though the claim that
one's Muse if feminine is rarely, if ever, unreservedly empowering or
positive, Milton gradually shows that his Muse is a woman.

In the first two proems, Milton carefully refers to the Muse in gender-
neutral terms: 'Sing Heav'nly Muse, that on the secret top / Of *Oreb*, or
of *Sinai*, didst inspire / That shepherd' (1. 6–8), 'Hail holy Light, ofspring
of Heav'n first born, / Or of th'Eternal Coeternal beam' (3. 1–2), and
'hear'st thou rather pure Ethereal stream, / Whose Fountain who shall
tell? Before the Sun, / Before the Heavens thou wert' (3. 7–9). In the
proem to Book 7, however, Milton reveals two crucial pieces of information. While he may be uncertain about her identity, he knows the
power which dictates to him nightly is female: 'Descend from Heav'n
Urania, by that name / If rightly thou art call'd' (7. 1–2). Furthermore,
Urania's previous company is also female: 'Thou with Eternal wisdom
didst converse / Wisdom thy sister' (7. 9–10). Whereas up to Book 6
Milton refers to her as either 'Heaven'ly Muse' or 'holy light,' terms
that gave no indication either way of gender, now he calls her 'Goddess'
(7. 40). In the proem to Book 9, Milton famously disclaims responsibility for *Paradise Lost*, basing his claim for authority entirely on the
poem's divine origin. May the poem fail, Milton asserts, 'if all be mine, /

Not Hers who brings it nightly to my Ear' (9. 46–7). The divine author, Milton insists, is a woman, and Milton refers to himself as her passive, female vessel. In a poem where all the authority figures are emphatically masculine (God, Adam, Satan, Michael, Raphael), Milton feminizes the poetic imagination, transforming his own dependence on women.

Milton does more than project a fantasy of his ideal relationship with a woman, the Muse providing what his daughters manifestly do not. As with his politics and theology, how Milton's views on gender appear in the poem are widely debated (Wittreich 1994, McColley 1983, Nyquist 1987). My account points up how the circumstances of composition, the dependence on female readers enforced on Milton, make the female Muse more striking. It also echoes in Adam's demand for a spouse with whom he can converse rationally. This had been anticipated by Milton's definition of the ideal marriage in *Doctrine and Discipline of Divorce*, where marriage is defined as 'the apt and cheerfull conversation of man with woman, to comfort and refresh him against the evil of solitary life' (935). Adam likewise tells God that while the Father maybe perfect, 'not so is Man, / But in degree, the cause of his desire / By conversation with his like to help' (8. 416–18). Yet God gives Adam something very different. In place of a partner 'fit to partic-ipate / [in] All rational delight' (8. 389–90), God gives Adam a highly sexualized creature that, for Adam, destroys all rational delight: 'All higher knowledge in her presence falls / Degraded, Wisdom in discourse with her / Looses discount'nanc't, and like folly shews' (8. 551–3).

Critics go on to argue whether Adam is right on this point, and whether his conclusions are typical of other readings of Genesis in the period. Their arguments, though, gain something when considered against Milton's reliance for his creativity on daughters who might or might not read out the relevant portions of books he needed to consult, read them out correctly, read them out with feeling. Those daughters might, after all, be wondering with Eve as she ponders over whether to share the apple with an Adam who doubts her ability, whether to

> give him to partake
> Full happiness with mee, or rather not,
> But keep the odds of Knowledge in my power
> Without Copartner? So to add what wants
> In femal Sex, the more to draw his Love,
> And render me more equal, and perhaps,
> A thing not undesireable, sometime
> Superior; for inferior who is free? (9. 818–25)

It suggests that nineteenth-century artists were not wholly wrong to show both blindness and femininity as vital elements in Milton's creative environment. Milton imported the confusion reigning in the political realm into his poem through the profusion of contradictory accounts and claims. Conversely, rather than reflecting the domestic hostility surrounding him in his portrayal of Eve, Milton transmutes this environment into a critical reflection on the matter of gender, a glimmering recognition of frustration on the part of his daughters, if not the Muse herself. Milton did not rise above his circumstances – he used them.

Works Cited

Coleridge, Samuel Taylor, 1950. 'Milton (1818),' in James Thorpe, ed., *Milton Criticism: Selections from Four Centuries*. New York: Rinehart.

Danielson, Dennis, 1982. *Milton's Good God: A Study in Literary Theodicy*. Cambridge and New York: Cambridge University Press.

Darbishire, Helen, ed., 1932. *The Early Lives of Milton*. London: Constable.

Gilbert, Sandra, 1978. 'Patriarchal Poetry and Women Readers: Reflections on Milton's Bogey,' *PMLA*, 93 (1978): 368–82.

Helgerson, Richard, 1983. *Self-Crowned Laureates: Spenser, Jonson, Milton and the Literary System*. Berkeley: University of California Press.

Herman, Peter C., 2006. *Destabilizing Milton: 'Paradise Lost' and the Poetics of Incertitude*. New York: Palgrave.

Lewalski, Barbara, 2003. *The Life of John Milton*. Rev. edn. Oxford: Blackwell.

Maus, Katharine E., 1995. *Inwardness and Theater in the English Renaissance*. Chicago: University of Chicago Press.

McColley, Diane, 1983. *Milton's Eve*. Urbana: University of Illinois Press.

Milton, John, 1953–82. *Complete Prose Works of John Milton*, ed. Don M. Wolfe. 8 vols. New Haven: Yale University Press.

Milton, John, 1998. *The Riverside Milton*, ed. Roy Flannagan. Houghton Mifflin: Boston.

Newlyn, Lucy, 1993. *'Paradise Lost' and the Romantic Reader*. Oxford: Clarendon Press.

Nyquist, Mary, 1987. 'The Genesis of Gendered Subjectivity in the Divorce Tracts and in *Paradise Lost*,' in Mary Nyquist and Margaret W. Ferguson, eds, *Re-Membering Milton: Essays on the Texts and Traditions*. New York: Methuen.

Sauer, Elizabeth, 1996. *Barbarous Dissonance and Images of Voice in Milton's Epics*. Montreal: McGill-Queens University Press.

Sidney, Philip, 2001. *Sir Philip Sidney's 'An Apology for Poetry' and 'Astrophil and Stella': Texts and Contexts*, ed. Peter C. Herman. Glen Allen, VA: College Publishing.

Wittreich, Joseph, 1994. '"Inspir'd with Contradiction": Mapping Gender Discourses in *Paradise Lost*,' in Diana T. Benet and Michael Lieb, eds, *Literary Milton: Text, Pretext, Context*. Pittsburgh: Duquesne University Press.

Woolf, Virginia, 1979. *The Diary*, ed. A. O. Bell. New York: Harcourt Brace Jovanovich.

Literary Heritage: Stratford and the Globe

Conversation: FARAH KARIM-COOPER
and KATE RUMBOLD

KR: I'm the Research Fellow at the Shakespeare Institute, where I co-ordinate the AHRC project 'Interrogating Cultural Value in the Twenty-first century: the Case of Shakespeare'. The project explores Shakespeare's contemporary value in compulsory education, publicly funded theatre and literary heritage.

FKC: And I'm the Head of Courses and Research in Globe Education at Shakespeare's Globe.

KR: Could we start by thinking about whether the Globe and Stratford offer different ideas of Shakespeare's creative environment as a writer. Do they represent a simple contrast between Shakespeare as native, English genius from the Stratford countryside, and Shakespeare as edgy, urban playwright working in London?

FKC: In our courses and research at the Globe, we try to situate Shakespeare as part of a conversation that was going on in London at the time about the theatre industry. He was just one of the voices. But not in Stratford, I think.

KR: Yes, the idea of Shakespeare as solitary genius is more prevalent in Stratford. It's an image that dates back to the eighteenth century, and the Shakespeare Jubilee of 1769, which invited visitors to Stratford to celebrate him and his natural, untutored Englishness. There isn't always an obvious connection between an author's birthplace and their literary output, and over the years Stratford had to work hard to make that connection, beyond just documenting the kinds of flowers, fields, and Warwickshire practices that Shakespeare might somehow have imbibed.

FKC: Does this affect what sort of expectations audiences bring when they come to Stratford?

KR: Yes, certainly. Stratford tries to get away from the forbidding figure of the lone, god-like writer to attract new visitors, but at the same time it has to trade on his high status in order to make people make the journey, make the pilgrimage into the countryside. The Royal Shakespeare Company, Shakespeare Birthplace Trust, and even the Shakespeare Institute have to work in both these ways.

FKC: So what sort of different Shakespeares do we get in London and Stratford? Do they offer different kinds of value? I'm thinking here about the idea of the Shakespeare effect; there's a pervasive sense of Shakespeare as something separate from the work itself which everybody wants a taste of ...

KR: ... what Diana Owen [director of the Birthplace Trust] refers to as the difficulty of getting your arms around Shakespeare, because 'he' is a free-floating idea and it's hard to convince people that your institution, be it in London or Stratford, is *the* place to go to experience 'Shakespeare.' In fact, each institution offers a very different 'Shakespeare,' each with a unique combination of symbolic values such as Englishness, history, heritage, education, prestige, entertainment, relevance, fun, and literary skill.

FKC: The notion of reconstructing the Globe is probably as utopian as it sometimes feels, but it's what we use, and is the most obvious draw to Shakespeare. You hear people walking by saying, 'Oh, that's the Globe – that's where he wrote his plays – he actually performed here,' so there's also a myth that this is the actual Globe. We don't even do 'original practices' productions any more, but the general public are not aware of that.

KR: The idea that if you can be close to the actors you can somehow be close to Shakespeare, you can cross the divide, is a construction that's a compelling fantasy for theatre companies and audiences alike. For instance, the Royal Shakespeare Theatre is being rebuilt at Stratford with a new thrust stage.

FKC: At the Globe, we literally trade on this fantasy – you can get your own bit of Shakespeare, take him home with you! I ask my students to talk about Shakespeare as a product, then we walk around the gift shop with its bizarre objects with Shakespeare's face on them or quotations, scarves and nick-nacks ...

KR: … a brand that sells! All the institutions, the RSC, Birthplace, and the Globe, deal with that overlap between presenting Shakespeare as theatre and presenting Shakespeare as heritage, and define themselves somewhere on that spectrum.

FKC: The Globe was created by Sam Wanamaker specifically because there was no heritage site dedicated to Shakespeare in London. Criticism about the Globe often ends up with accusations about museum theatre in a re-enactment-park, which is viewed as criticism by theatre artists who are, in their minds, creating lively, current, and dynamic theatre – though the defence, of course, is that this is new acting, not re-enacting.

KR: The Birthplace Trust is trying to use theatre to get away from the sorts of baggage that go with Merrie England, and to heighten visitors' sense of connection with 'Shakespeare.' Shakespeare's Birthplace and Anne Hathaway's Cottage are the two most-visited of the properties; the other less famous properties [Nash's House and New Place, Hall's Croft, where his daughter and son-in-law lived; Mary Arden's House, childhood home of Shakespeare's mother; and Harvard House, which is preserved as an example of an Elizabethan house] are increasingly devising strategies, such as participatory events, to attract visitors. Mary Arden's House is now a working farm, for example. They've put live actors into the houses to come out and regale visitors with bits of speeches from the plays. They're also reorganizing their exhibitions – less trudging around the different boards on the wall and more dramatic encounters with selected items, more 'ta-da' moments when you encounter a different artefact from Shakespeare's time.

FKC: Do you think this is a response to our digital culture, to audiences which expect more participation and interactivity?

KR: Yes, at the micro and the macro levels. There's been a big move in cultural funding policy towards the idea that the public should decide which institutions deserve public money, and how they should be run. But there's also a shift, theoretically, in tourism studies. Partly in response to new digital technologies, theorists are locating authenticity not in the place which you visit but in the experience of the tourist. You can have an authentic experience anywhere. This might give heritage tourists more creative licence, but it presents a challenge for the building-based institutions trying to attract them. Do you think it is a challenge or an opportunity for the Globe?

FKC: When they were building the theatre, the Globe trustees wanted it to be as authentic as possible, but only in terms of the building materials and building methods. Yet the word is still thrown at the Globe from time to time. Andrew Gurr refers to the construction itself as a 'best guess,' because there are still a lot of features that are inauthentic, as it were, in that we just don't know how everything was done four hundred years ago. Then Mark Rylance and his artistic team started producing 'original practices' productions, where they researched the cultural practices of the Elizabethan world and, specifically, the theatre companies' material practices. For instance, Jenny Tiramani applied the same principles that Sam Wanamaker applied to the reconstruction of the building, to use dress fabrics that were available in this period. We may not know whether or not the companies used them but we know that they were available to them.

KR: The Birthplace has been carefully rescued but it's also been fabricated. It's worked with what is authentic and what makes it feel like it's authentic, as in the case of the interior decoration. It's a fudging that has gone on there since it was bought in the 1840s. The RSC's theatre reconstruction has the same mixture of old and new – English Heritage has praised it as a good example of 'constructive conservation,' because the older theatre is a heritage building in its own right. In production terms, the RSC is more free from the authenticity requirement; indeed, making Shakespeare our contemporary is its tag-line. Even so, some audience members walk out of what they see as shockingly modern versions of productions.

FKC: An RSC designer told me that the Courtyard theatre [the current temporary structure used while rebuilding the main theatre] was a response to the Globe's design. Meanwhile, our new artistic director here [Dominic Dromgoole] wants to bring the Globe into modernity more fully by asking playwrights now to write plays for the space, as well as doing very contemporary productions of Shakespeare. Is the RSC coming our way, while we move yours?

KR: In terms of physical structure, the RSC's Swan theatre, with its thrust stage, preceded the London Globe so this isn't a simple story of adoption. But I think we can see some of the ethos of the Globe's practice being employed. The RSC is interested in two key ideas behind original practices: audience interaction, which you can see in many recent productions, and ensemble work. They used an ensemble for the 2006–8 History Cycle, and now the RSC describes itself as an 'ensemble company,' where all members of staff, be they directors or producers or admin or workshop staff, all 'collaborate' in their approach to theatre.

FKC: There are myths about a rivalry between the Lord Chamberlain's men and the Lord Admiral's men, and perhaps the same kind of myth exists between the RSC and Globe now. When Dominic Dromgoole first announced that we wouldn't be doing 'original practices' productions, there was some concern that it would just be RSC at the Globe, missing some ingredient, some authenticity. A number of directors and actors move between the two, of course.

KR: So less polarization, less RSC/establishment vs Globe/maverick?

FKC: Patrick Spottiswoode [Director of Globe Education] would argue that we're still maverick in that we're not government subsidized, so there is a kind of freedom …

KR: … but perhaps because the Globe has been in existence for some years now, it will start to seem more mainstream?

FKC: It may look like the Globe is quite corporate, given its reliance upon that sort of sponsorship. Increasingly, our most innovative projects in Globe Education, such as 'Playing Shakespeare with Deutsche Bank,' produced by my colleague, Christopher Stafford in Learning, are funded by major corporations. But this funding enables the Globe project as a whole and Globe Education specifically to do the work that was originally envisioned for it by our founder, Sam Wanamaker. I think when we see the gift shop and the café-restaurant, the renting of the Exhibition for corporate events, there is more danger there of being perceived of as 'corporate Shakespeare.' But even those enterprises are part and parcel of the Globe's identity as a 'centre.' A place where people come to see, read, study, workshop, learn about, talk about Shakespeare is also a place where people can buy stuff, eat, drink, and participate in events. It enables, again, the whole project to continue doing its work of producing important learning and research projects, as well as meaningful Shakespearean and non-Shakespearean performances.

KR: The RSC would argue that public funding gives it freedom to innovate: to put on short runs of plays and to try out new material. It also brings responsibilities of accountability, of hitting certain social and educational targets. I think education in particular comes in here. Both institutions have a very strong educational component: the RSC works with students and teachers of all ages and recently launched its 'Stand up for Shakespeare' manifesto for Shakespeare in schools. What kind of creative environments do you think the Globe and Stratford offer for study and research?

FKC: We've divided Globe Education into Learning [for schools], Events, Courses [university and conservatory training programmes], and Research. The Globe Research team is largely staffed by volunteers, particularly PhD student interns, and two Collaborative Doctoral Award students who benefit from a kind of young scholar mentoring programme. In particular, they get privileged access, which they wouldn't get anywhere else, to be honest, because we have a theatre department which is willing to work with the young academics and which wants lectures during rehearsals. We have actors here who are hungry for information and students anxious to hear about acting experience in relation to their topics. But research at the Globe isn't confined to the dramaturgical support during the rehearsal process – the performance practice at the Globe, audiences, writing, and theatre space are all unique areas of enquiry here. We are researching non-Shakespearean drama as well, particularly looking for ways to uncover what has been learned through Globe Education's Read Not Dead series of staged readings. Actors who participate in these readings each season have a great deal to share with our researchers about the process of performing non-Shakespearean drama, and just being able to see and hear these, often obscure, plays staged enables our researchers and PhD students to gain a comprehensive sense of the way in which early modern drama operated in conversation with Shakespearean drama. Sometimes it is not always easy to tell how the research we do affects the productions, but actors very frequently talk about how their approach was deeply affected or inspired by what we tell them and we have had directors who have thought of us as indispensable during the planning stages.

KR: Seeing the outcomes of their research on stage so quickly must be extraordinary for them. At Stratford, we've got the archives of the RSC, the Shakespeare Centre library, and the Institute's own dedicated Shakespeare library as resources, so there's the potential – sometimes taken up, sometimes not – for researchers to work on the interface between literary criticism, heritage, and theatre.

FKC: Yes – mixing up the disciplines is difficult. I think there is a suspicion that popularizing Shakespeare de-aestheticizes the work. Some of our audiences have been compared to crowds at football matches and rock concerts – actually, a few rock bands have asked to launch their albums in the Globe. I think what this suggests is that Shakespearean performance at the Globe is on a rather massive scale like an event; open and broad and loud.

KR: And there's still that self-consciousness about mixing high and low Shakespeare. It's not as straightforward as going to a match or gig, because you're aware of that deliberate clash, and – like audiences of *Macbeth: Kill Bill Shakespeare*, which mixed Shakespeare and Tarantino – perhaps even sometimes baffled by it.

FKC: If you type in 'Shakespeare and performance' on YouTube you come up with all sorts of Shakespeares, from Lego Shakespeare to the Beatles doing the rude mechanicals scene to *The Merchant of Venice* meets Star Wars. But it's all Shakespeare; it's what performance scholars have called remixing Shakespeare …

KR: … even multiplying 'Shakespeares' …

FKC: … all the way to using Shakespeare to construct new plays. At the Globe a brilliant new play, *Frontline*, debuted this season. Its author, Che Walker, was part of the Globe company in 2007, in Wilson Milam's production of *Othello*. Walker played small parts, a bit like Shakespeare, but got a direct sense of the Globe audience and the stage's spatial language. During the run of *Othello*, he wrote his own modern tragedy about life in Camden town.

KR: We find that about the Stratford environment when it comes to new writing. The Other Place [now part of the Courtyard Theatre] was used to provide experimental space for new work alongside the main theatres, and the Complete Works of Shakespeare Festival [2006–7] featured a number of new plays. There are several posts for writers in residence at the RSC, from working as dramaturges in the rehearsal room to writing new plays inspired by the season's theme. The writers talk about getting immersion in a period's language, in an ensemble technique, and, in the case of the history cycle, immersion in a theme. The RSC encourages writers to make creative use of these, rather than simply adapting or reviving Shakespeare's plays in a new form. For example, one International Writer in Residence, Adriano Shapiro, said that he had little experience of Shakespeare he when arrived at RSC, but it gave him the chance to see a group of artists puzzling over his work, and to tune into the language. He said it helped him understand the 'recipe' that Shakespeare used for turning history into dramatic story-telling, and that he's used it as a 'blueprint' for his own new history play, *The Tragedy of Thomas Hobbes*, which is based on the Enlightenment's concerns.

FKC: Does that happen in your own research?

KR: Generally – and obviously – working close to a theatre company encourages greater emphasis on performance practice; getting away from text-centred ideas of 'Shakespeare,' and opening eyes to the theatre practices, such as collaboration, that would have shaped his work. More unusually, though, the 'interrogating cultural value' project has been doing some interesting work with RSC marketing. The Company uses sophisticated software to find out the make-up of their audiences, and working with them has told us more about the kind of audiences that engage with Shakespeare today. We've also examined the language of value that's used to market him to contemporary audiences. So it benefits both the research and the theatre company.

Tavern and Library: Working with Ben Jonson

MICHELLE O'CALLAGHAN and ADAM SMYTH

STUDIES OF THE MATERIALITY of textual practice tend to concentrate on publication and transmission: either the mechanisms and formats of text in press, or the composition, circulation, and consumption of texts in scribal cultures. For instance, despite its title Roger Chartier's recent *Inscription and Erasure: Literature and Written Culture from the Eleventh to the Eighteenth Century* concentrates not on the act of inscription, but what happens after the words are on the page. Hence, it is the publication process that is the primary site of his investigation of the 'transactions between works of literature and the social world' (Chartier 2007, ix). One difficulty is that documentation of the everyday, domestic details of creative acts is scant. For instance, Richard Daborne, collaborating with Philip Massinger and Nathan Field, merely tells Henslowe that they spent 'a great deale of Time in conference about [the] plot' (Nochimson 2002, 51).

With a few notable exceptions, less attention has been paid to the creative act itself, to the transactions between the material and the textual in the moment when the hand puts pen to paper, and the physical environment and technologies that make it possible for writing to take place. Why is work-a-day detail of creative processes so difficult to find, say, in letters and other writings of early modern authors? Perhaps partly because authors, as Chartier notes, devoted their energies not to recording their creative lives but to transforming 'the material realities of writing and publication into an aesthetic resource' (Chartier 2007, x, xii). We do find writing objects and publishing technologies in literary texts, but they frequently have undergone a transmutation, and have been turned into a metaphorical storehouse. On the one hand, pens, paper, ink, and so forth, appear as metonyms for the material creative environment; on the other, they can be transformed into metaphors which argue that the literary work transcends its material existence.

Ben Jonson is distinctive because he did leave records of his creative practices. His poems and plays, his *Discoveries*, and remembrances and letters of contemporaries and near-contemporaries – including William Drummond, Lucius Cary, Viscount Falkland, James Howell,

John Aubrey, and Thomas Fuller – are a rich repository of Jonson's meditations on writing and of details of his habits when at work.

Scenes of Writing

Describing his library, Michel de Montaigne said:

> I try to make my authority over it absolute, and to withdraw this one corner from all society, conjugal, filial, and civic ... Sorry the man, to my mind, who has not in his own home a place to be all by himself, to pay his court privately to himself, to hide!
>
> (Montaigne 1958, 629)

While it would be misleading to take Montaigne's description of solitary withdrawal too literally – on his chair ('my throne'), amid his books, he was still surrounded by secretaries as well as visitors (West 2004, 116) – Montaigne's description is nevertheless a potent expression of one idea of authorship. In his vignette, authorship is figured in terms of absolute authority and withdrawal; writerly self-fulfilment proceeds, Montaigne suggests, through a separation from society. The private space of his own room is an objective correlative of the new individualized consciousness with which Montaigne is linked. Could this be the scene of early modern authorship?

In some ways Jonson conforms to this image of authorship. Narratives of Jonson as author, by Jonson himself and rearticulated by modern critics, construct a remarkable *individual*. His role in creating a nascent idea of authorship and his revolutionary use of print to stabilize a writer's corpus (Loewenstein 2002) might make one expect a creative process concerned with the forceful expression of an individual's will, exerting absolute authority over the place and process of making. However, despite a post-Romantic tendency to conceive of the author as a solitary, even lonely figure, Jonson's writing often attests to creativity as a collaborative process. When, in 'The Execration Upon Vulcan,' Jonson laments the writings he lost in the 1623 fire that consumed 'my desk,' he remembers the labour and help (in the form of friends lending books) that produced his writings, 'Wherein was Oil, beside the Succour spent, / Which Noble Carew, Cotton, Selden lent.' In Blackfriars in the early 1600s, Jonson was a neighbour of his former schoolfellow at Westminster school, Sir Robert Cotton, when the latter was living at Lord Hunsdon's house. The house, and its library in particular, was a meeting place in London for poets and antiquaries – Jonson, Samuel Daniel, Michael Drayton, John Donne, and Hugh Holland – so much so that Holland described it as 'the Randevouse of all good and honeste spirits so it seemed a kind of universitie.' Later, in the 1620s, Jonson was one of the regular visitors at Cotton's house and library at Westminster (Sharpe 1979, 202–3, 212). The library was an important site for creativity in the early modern period, not necessarily because, as Montaigne enthused, it provided a secluded space within the crowded household for the author's private withdrawal 'from all society,' but because it could also provide a physical environment for and a symbol of the intellectual exchanges of like-minded men. Jonson's Epigram LXXXVI praising Sir Henry Goodyere's 'wel-made choise of friends, and bookes' turns on the chiasmus of 'making thy friends bookes, and thy bookes friends' (Jonson 1975, 61).

The text of *Sejanus* performed on stage (to rather unimpressed audiences) was the product of Jonson and an unnamed 'second: pen,' 'so happy a genius' who 'had good share' in the writing. When Jonson came to revise the text for print in 1605, he removed this co-author's writing, choosing rather 'to put weaker, and no doubt, less pleasing [words], of mine own, than to defraud so happy a genius of his right by my loathed usurpation' ('To the Readers,' Jonson 1932b, 351). But this revised *Sejanus* retained a strong spirit of collaboration through the several prefatory verses that framed the play: what Jonson called the 'following and voluntary labours of my friends,' who included George Chapman, John Marston, Hugh Holland, and William Strachey. Jonson's poetry, too, is enmeshed in dialogue: he sent his epigrams to Donne, for example, to receive the latter's editorial approval. Epigram XCVI asks him to 'Read all I send: and, if I find but one / Marked by thy hand … / My title's sealed' (Jonson 1975, 67–8). According to William Drummond, Jonson 'thinketh nothing well what either he himself or some of his friends and countrymen hath said or done.'

Jonson's literary friendships were often cast in terms of consanguinity. The Sons (or Tribe) of Ben was a loose, patrilineal community where the literary sociability of the circle, academy, or school was turned into a kind of family, dependent on self-styled father Ben. In 'An Eclogue on the Death of Ben. Iohnson,' Lucius Cary describes how Jonson will be memorialized by a collaboration between author and heirs:

> … from the *Academies, Courts,* and *Townes*;
> Let *Digby Carew, Killigrew,* and *Maine,*
> *Godolphin, Waller,* that inspired *Traine,*

Or whose rare *Pen* beside deserves the *grace*,
Or of an *equall*, or a neighbouring *Place*,
Answer thy *wish*, for none so fit appears
To raise his *Tombe*, as who are left his *Heires*:
Yet for this *Cause* no labour need be spent,
Writing his *Workes*, he built his *Monument*.
(*Jonsonus Virbius* 1638, 8)

The conventional link between authorship and fatherhood becomes, in Jonson's verse, a refrain, from the epigram that marks the death of his son Ben, aged seven (the child is described as Jonson's 'best piece of poetry'), to 'the Memory of My Beloved, the Author Mr William Shakespeare: And What He Hath Left Us,' where Jonson tells the reader to 'Look how the father's face / Lives in his issue' (Jonson 1975, 48, 265).

When Jonson writes that his title is 'seal'd' by the mark that he hopes Donne will place against one of his poems, he is punning on the seal as a physical object – the device with an heraldic or emblematic design that is impressed onto a piece of wax on a document, which lay on the desk alongside the writing instruments – or the wax itself, which functions as evidence of authorization. The imagined seal affirms Donne's estimation of the quality of Jonson's verse and is a sign of their literary friendship. While this seems to be a rare show of humility on Jonson's part, it actually incorporates Donne into his system of quality assurance. The seal appears again in 'An Epistle Answering to One that Asked to be Sealed of the Tribe of Ben' (*Underwoods*, Jonson 1975, 47). Again, 'sealed' has the sense of being stamped with a mark as guarantee of authenticity, perhaps the sealed licence or badge of a company or guild, in this case, the 'Tribe of Ben.' In his verse epistle 'To his noble ffather, Mr. Jonson,' Lucius Cary referred to three meetings at which he witnessed the 'force' of this literary 'Lion' before he had the courage to write his own epistle, and so put himself forward for the title of a Son of Ben (Jonson 1952, XI. 402–4). It is possible that the prospective son petitioned for adoption through verse, which was then returned with Jonson's wax seal or some other mark as a sign of critical approval, authenticating the son's verse as bearing the stamp of its father.

The wax of the seal was put to a different use in Jonson's early play *Every Man Out of His Humour*, as a sign of authoritative poetic censure. Carlo Buffone, a 'scurrilous, and profane jester,' is a figure for the bad poet or, more specifically, the malicious satirist. At the close of Act 5, scene 3, set at the Mitre tavern, Puntarvolo and Macilente hold down Buffone and seal his mouth with wax. John Pell told Aubrey that Buffone was based on 'one Charles Chester ... a perpetuall talker [who] ... made a noyse like a drumme in a roome. So, one time at a taverne, Sir Walter Ralegh beates him and seales-up his mouth i.e. his upper and neather beard with hard-wax. From him Ben Johnson takes his Jester in *Everyman out of his Humour*' (Aubrey 2000, 265; Steggle 1999). Here, lips are sealed into silence. Literary censure hardens into censorship.

While Jonson's creativity is dependent upon forms of collaboration, his writing is haunted by two figures of anti-community: the plagiarist and the poor reader. His 'son,' Lucius Cary, who had been sealed by the father, was authorized to 'steal' from his 'father.' Cary said of his poem marking the anniversary of the death of Henry Morrison that 'What here is ill in them, (w[hi]ch I feare is all) it belongs only to my self; if there be any thing tolerable, it is somethinge you [Jonson] drop't negligentlie some day at the Dogg, & I tooke up' (Jonson 1952, XI. 400). However, the writer who employs 'old ends ... To stop gaps in his loose writing'; who makes 'his play [from] ... iests, stolne from each table' ('Prologue,' *Volpone*, Jonson 1937b, 24) is a very different matter – he corrupts collaboration. In *Poetaster* Jonson ridicules the recycling in conversation of stolen lines: 'I got that speech by seeing a play last day, and it did me some grace now: I see, 'tis good to collect sometimes; I'le frequent these plays more' (2. 2, Jonson 1932a, 229). The plagiarist, the 'Poet-Ape' (who gets an epigram to himself, Epigram LVI, Jonson 1975, 51), offends Jonson's emerging sense of literary ownership, affronts the pursuit of artistic coherence ('For as in an instrument, so in style, there must be a harmony and consent of parts' [*Discoveries*, Jonson 1975, 426]), and distorts the kind of community upon which his writing was based. Plagiarism, for Jonson, was a breach of social etiquette. Similarly, the figure of the poor reader, so frequently invoked by Jonson, is the inverse of the close friend or Son. Jonson distinguished between a bad reader ('a pretender,' often 'cozened' ['To the Reader,' *Alchemist*, Jonson 1937a, 291], 'Who scarce can spell th' hard names' [Epigram III, Jonson 1975, 35], who is prone to 'Application' and 'who profess[es] to have a key for the decyphering of every thing' ['The Epistle,' *Volpone*, Jonson 1937b, 18–19]), and the 'understander' who actively seeks out good writing ('If thou beest more, thou art an understander, and then I trust thee' ['To the Reader,' *The Alchemist*, Jonson 1937a, 291]). Jonson's cultures of collaboration and understanding were threatened by the plagiarist and the poor reader.

'In flowing measure': Taverns and Creativity

It is Jonson, more than any other early modern poet, whose creativity is associated with the tavern and who is a key figure in the transformation of the tavern into one of the homes of the English Renaissance Muses. His name has long been associated with the Mermaid tavern on Bread Street, near the corner of Old Fish Street and the stairs to the Thames, and Jonson consecrated his own room, the Apollo Room, at the Devil and St Dunstan tavern on Fleet Street. Together with his Sons he frequented other taverns in London: Herrick in his *Hesperides* remembered those '*Lyrick* Feasts, / Made at the *Sun*, / The *Dog*, the triple *Tunne*' (Herrick 1921, 282), and in *Bartholomew Fair* Littlewit compares his own inventions to 'these Pretenders to Wit! Your Three Cranes, Miter and Mermaid men!' (1. 1, Jonson 1938, 20).

The tavern, like other drinking houses, was a social hub (Clark 1983; Kümin and Tlusty 2002). Drinking houses were one of the few substantial communal spaces outside the household and public institutions (churches, courts, universities) where individuals could meet regularly and socialize, as well as eat and drink, without a familial or professional affiliation to the place. Hence, the tavern, like the later coffee houses, fostered the formation and proliferation of voluntary organizations and societies. The tavern from the latter part of the sixteenth century was increasingly identified with a specific cultural activity: writing plays and poetry (Smyth 2004; O'Callaghan 2007, 65–70). Actors socialized with members of the audience at taverns. Plays and 'books' were read and performed. Stephen Gosson in his *School of Abuse* (1579) wrote approvingly of 'the two prose books played at the Belsavage, where you shall find never a word without wit.' The tavern was the scene both of collective reading, the 'talked book' (Chartier 1989), and of collaborative composition. Playwrights met at taverns to compose plays. Jasper Mayne, in his elegy for Jonson, says teasingly,

> That such *thy drought* was, and so great *thy thirst*,
> That all thy *Playes* were *drawne* at th'*Mermaid* first
> (*Jonsonus Virbius* 1638, 30)

Thomas Fuller relates the anecdote in his *History* (1662) that Fletcher and Beaumont, 'Meeting once in a Tavern, to contrive the rude draught of a Tragedy, Fletcher undertook to kill the King therein, whose words being over-heard by a listener (though his Loyalty not be blamed herein) he was accused of High Treason, till the mistake soon appearing, that the plot was onely against Drammatick and Scenical King, all wound off in a merriment' (Fuller 1662, sig. Oooo1v). Moreover, bits of plays performed on stage became bits of wit performed in the tavern, and, as Jonson complained, jests let fly at the table ended up in plays. Thomas Nabbes similarly pointed to those 'that from the Poets labours gather notes ... for th'exercise of wit / At Taverns' (Nabbes 1637, sig. A3v).

Although Jonson is identified with the apotheosis of the tavern into the place of 'Lyrick feasts,' it appears in his early plays as a negative *locus* for a type of sub-literary production. In *Every Man in His Humour* (1601), the Mitre tavern on Bread Street is the scene of extemporized versifying:

> *Prospero*: Signior *Matheo*, who made these verses? they are excellent good.
> *Matheo*: Oh God sir, its your pleasure to say so sir. Fayth I made them *extempore* this morning.
> *Prospero*: How *extempore*?
> *Matheo*: I would I might be damd els: aske signior *Bobadillo*. He sawe me write them, at the: (poxe on it) the *Miter* yonder
> (3. 4, Jonson 1927, 249–50)

Extemporized versification in company was valued as a form of *sprezzatura*, showing the composer possessed a quick wit that was natural and not forced. This is a spoken and performative rather than written discourse. Yet though immediacy demonstrates rhetorical mastery and a powerful memory, it can also be a dissipation of accumulated knowledge. 'Writing is a mode of conservation, whereas the improvident tongue is always tempted by prodigality' (Cave 1985, 127, 139–40). Jonson gives a negative characterization of extemporization because he privileges the written, with its powers of conservation, over the spoken. Extemporized tavern poetry bridges the written and the spoken and performed, and is a particularly ephemeral and quick mode of writing. These sets of associations are at work in George Puttenham's description of the epigram, which

> is but an inscription or writing made as it were upon a table, or in a window, or upon the wall or mantel of a chimney in some place of common resort, where it was allowed every man might come, or be sitting to chat and prate, as now in our taverns and common tabling houses, where many merry heades meete, and scribe with inke, with chalk, or with a coal. (Puttenham 2007, 142)

In the early stages of his career, Jonson himself was identified with this dissipated, quick and sharp-witted form of epigrammatic tavern composition (O'Callaghan 2007, 65–6). Thomas Dekker accused Jonson in 1602 of acting like his own Carlo Buffone when he 'supp[ed] at Tauernes, amongst [his] betters' and enjoined him 'not to dippe your Manners in too much sawce, nor at Table to fling Epigrams, Embleames, or Play-speeches about you (lyke Hayle-Stones) to keep you out of the terrible daunger of the Shot' (*Satiromasix* 5. 2, Dekker 1970, 383). Some sense of this Jonson, flinging out wit and insults, is conveyed in Drummond's description of 'a great lover and praiser of himself, a contemner and scorner of others, given rather to lose a friend than a jest, jealous of every word and action of those about him … he is passionately kind and angry, careless either to gain or keep, vindictive, but, if he be well answered, at himself' (*Conversations*, Jonson 1975, 479). Howell gossips about Jonson's table etiquette, in particular, a supper given by Jonson which was marred because Jonson 'began to engross all the discourse, to vapour extremely of himself, and by vilifying others to magnify his own muse' ('Letter to Sir Tho. Hawk, Knight, 5 April 1626,' Howell 1892, II. 403–4).

It was also said that Jonson more seriously transgressed a cardinal rule that governed dinner, that what was said at table, stayed at table, by drawing his characters not from his storehouse of learning but from his own drinking companions. Jasper Mayne's elegy for Jonson half-heartedly countered the charge made against Jonson 'that when *thou* in *company* wert met, / Thy *meate* took *notes*, and *thy discourse* was *net*' (*Jonsonus Virbius* 1638, 31). Plutarch, read widely in the period, explained that the proverb 'I dislike a drinking-companion with a good memory' alluded to the 'amnesty for all that is said and done during the drinking' (Plutarch 1969, 5). There is evidence that Jonson did draw, broadly, from the figures around him in his daily life. In his discussion of Shakespeare, Aubrey wrote that 'Ben Johnson and he did gather Humours of men dayly where ever they came.' For instance, the astrologer John Dee 'used to distill Egge-shells: and 'twas from hence that Ben Johnson had his hint of the Alkimist, whom he meant,' and Thomas Sutton (perhaps the richest commoner in England at the time of his death in 1611) 'was very much upon Mortgages: and fed severall with hopes of being his Heire. 'Twas from him that Ben Johnson tooke his hint of the Fox: and by Seignioro Volpone is meant Sutton' (Aubrey 2000, 290, 369, 303, 265). The figure of Horace in *Poetaster* represents a version of Jonson – of Jonson seen through his own eyes – and this poet is described by Demetrius as 'a meere spunge; nothing but humours, and observation; he goes up and downe sucking from every societie, and when hee comes home, squeazes himself drie again. I know him, I' (4. 3, Jonson 1932, 269). Horace himself says Virgil's poetry is 'ramm'd with life' (5. 1, Jonson 1932a, 293). The same could be said for Jonson's.

Jonson's response to the dissipation of tavern poetry was to translate its characteristically quick and convivial wit into the time-honoured motif of a symposium. Francis Beaumont, remembering the convivial times had with Jonson at the Mermaid tavern, invoked the classical association between wine and wit:

> what things have we seen
> Done at the Mermaid? Hard words that have been
> So nimble, and so full of subtill flame,
> As if that every one from whence they came
> Had meant to put his whole wit in a Jest,
> And had resolv'd to live a foole the rest
> Of his dull life (Beaumont 1660, sig. L6r–v)

The tavern had a monopoly on the sale of wine, which set it apart in class terms from the lower-class alehouse, which was restricted to beer and ale. This commercial and social distinction was transformed into an aesthetic distinction, which meant that the alehouse and the tavern came to signify different social models of creativity. Beaumont's witty tavern is one that comes from *vino veritas*: drinking good wine warms the brain, sharpens the intellect, and induces a state of poetic fury, akin to divine possession (O'Callaghan 2007, 68–9). In Epigram CI, Jonson wrote of this creative state of intoxication in 'Inviting a Friend to Supper':

> … that, which most doth take my *Muse*, and mee,
> Is a pure cup of rich *Canary*-wine,
>   Which is the *Mermaids*, now, but shall be mine:
> Of which had HORACE, or ANACREON tasted,
>   Their liues, as doe their lines, till now had lasted.
>   (Jonson 1975, 70)

Wine, the elixir of the gods, confers poetic immortality that makes the poet into a god. Jonson, in an epigram thanking Lucy Harington, Countess of Bedford, for the promise of a buck, sings 'Straight away went I home; and there most like a *Poet*, I fancied to my selfe, what wine, what wit / I would haue spent' (Epigram LXXXIV, Jonson 1975, 61). Intoxication, it seems, is the habitual state of the poet in the throes of creative activity. James Howell, in his letter 'To my Father Mr. Ben Iohnson,' plays on the notion of Jonson's creative 'madness' which is conceived within an Ovidian symposiastic rendering of *furor poeticus*:

> I find that you have been oftentimes mad; you were mad when you writ your *Fox*, and madder when you writ your *Alchimest*; you were mad when you writ your *Catilin*, and stark mad when you writ *Sejanus*; but when you writ your *Epigrams*, and the *Magnetic Lady*, you were not so mad, insomuch that I perceive there be degrees of madness in you. Excuse me that I am so free with you. The madness I mean, is that divine fury, that heating and heightening spirit which Ovid speaks of. (Howell 1892, 228)

Given the interdependency of divine fury and wine, Howell could also be implying that Jonson wrote his best work when intoxicated. This is certainly what Aubrey implies when he notes that Jonson 'would many times exceed in drinke, Canarie was his beloved liquor: then he would tumble home to bed; and when he had thoroughly perspired then to studie' (Aubrey 2000, 172). William Drummond described drink as 'one of the elements in which ... [Jonson] liveth' (*Conversations*, Jonson 1975, 479), and a verse remembering Jonson after his death noted that 'Sack was the Morning, Evening of thy name' (*Wit and Drollery* 1656, 79–80). 'Swell me a bowle with lustie wine,' says a Jonson-like Horace in *Poetaster*,

> Till I may see the plump LYAEVS swim
> Above the brim:
> I drinke, as I would wright,
> In flowing measure, fill'd with flame, and spright.
>   (3. 1, Jonson 1932a, 234)

When Jonson came to name the Apollo Room at the Devil and St Dunstan tavern in Fleet Street, he produced his own *Leges Convivales*, laws of feasting, which were engraved on a tablet over the fireplace.[1] The fact that they were inscribed in stone is telling. Where Puttenham described tavern poetry as scribbled with ink, chalk, or stone on any surface handy, Jonson gives his lines, which mark out his creative

---

[1] John Chamberlain included a copy of Jonson's *Leges Convivales* in a letter dated 19 June 1624, with the note that they were 'made for a faire roome or chamber lately built at the tavern or signe of the divell and St. Dunstan by Temple-barre' (Chamberlain 1939, II. 566).

possession of the Apollo Room, a physical monumentality. Here he picks up the cliché that verse lasts longer than stone, as in his epistle to Elizabeth, Countess of Rutland: 'Those other glorious notes, / Inscrib'd in touch or marble ... / doe but proue the wombs, / That bred them, graues' (*The Forrest*, Jonson 1975, 112). Jonson even had an epigram he made for Robert Cecil, Earl of Salisbury, in praise of his father, William, Lord Burleigh, engraved on a gold plate that was probably presented as a New Year's gift (*The Underwoods*, Jonson 1975, 168). Paper, as Jonson knew only too well, could burn, or end up as toilet paper, or, as he jested, be used to line pie tins, or to wrap vegetables at Bucklersbury market (Epigram III, Jonson 1975, 35). By appropriating the tools and material of the craftsmen as metaphors for his own poetic craft, Jonson conserves his creative acts.

The chair in which Jonson sat, and wrote, was an important creative prop. Aubrey recorded that 'I have seen his studyeing chaire, which was of strawe, such as old women use; and as Aulus Gellius is drawen in' (Aubrey 2000, 172). Jonson would have been pleased with the parallel with the Latin author Aulus Gellius, author of *Attic Nights*. This link between Jonson's chair and his classicism is reinforced in his drama: when, in *Poetaster*, Caesar asks Virgil to read from his *Aeneid*, he says, 'See then this Chair, of purpose set for thee / To read thy Poem in; refuse it not' (5. 2, Jonson 1932a, 295). Jonson's chair appears to have lived on as a relic at Robert Wilson's tavern in the Strand. In *Wit and Drollery* (1656), a verse celebration of Jonson is titled 'Verses written over the Chair of Ben: Johnson, now remaining at Robert Wilsons, at the signe of Johnson's head in the Strand' (79–80). And Edward Phillips's *The Mysteries of Love and Eloquence* (1658) includes the following jest:

Q   Why is Ben. Johnsons chair at Robert Wilsons Tipling-house in the Strand?
A   To signifie that Poets in these hard times, though they should invoke the nine Muses, may still want nine pence to purchase a pint of Canary. (Phillips 1658, question 164)

Given the centrality of drinking and eating to Jonson's writing life, it is not surprising that reading, writing, and creativity are often described through metaphors of consumption (Boehrer 1997). Jonson employed an apiarian metaphor popular among humanists to describe the appropriation of reading materials: 'draw forth out of the best and choicest flowers, with the bee, and turn all into honey, work it into one relish

and savour; make our imitation sweet' (*Discoveries*, Jonson 1975, 448).
In *Poetaster*, Horace declares: 'I drinke, as I would wright, / In flowing
measure, fill'd with flame, and spright' (III. 1, Jonson 1932a, 234), and
the dramatic preferences of audiences are described as 'the palates of
the season' ('Prologue,' *Volpone*, Jonson 1937b, 23). Poor writing, in
particular, is often described in terms of indigestion. The poet who
fails 'to convert the substance or riches of another poet to his own
use' is described as 'a creature that swallows what it takes in crude,
raw, or undigested' (*Discoveries*, Jonson 1975, 448). In *Poetaster*, Virgil
instructs Crispinus, who has vomited up a series of indigestible words,
to swallow 'A strict and wholesom Diet' of learning to cure his creative
indigestion:

> Looke, you take
> Each morning, of old CATOES principles
> A good draught, next your heart; that walke upon,
> Till it be well digested: Then come home,
> And taste a piece of TERENCE, sucke his phrase
> In stead of lycorice. (5. 3, Jonson 1932a, 314)

'*It shall go so*': *the Speed of Creativity*

And yet, despite all this convivial, collaborative, contingent composition, there is another side to Jonson's work. Opponents of Jonson often
mocked his supposedly slow rate of composition; they did 'Cry hoarsely
… when his playes come forth … With saying, he was a yeere about
them' ('Prologue,' *Volpone*, Jonson 1937b, 23–4). Thomas Dekker's *Satiromastix* (1602) presents Horace, a thinly disguised Jonson, composing
verse with a costive difficulty. Horace is 'sitting in a study behinde a
Curtaine, a candle by him burning, bookes lying confuesedly,' as he
battles to find his rhymes for 'an *Epithalamium* for Sir *Walter Terrels*
wedding':

> For I to thee and thine immortall name,
> In-in-in golden tunes,
> For I to thee and thine immortall name –
> In-sacred raptures flowing, flowing, swimming, swimming:
> In sacred raptures swimming,
> Immortall name, game, dame, tame, lame, lame, lame.
> (1. 2, Dekker 1970, 316)

Mayne repeated these criticisms in his memorial poem for *Jonsonus Virbius* in order to clear Jonson's name:

> Scorne then their censures, who gav't out, *thy Witt*
> As long upon a *Comoedie* did sit
> As *Elephants* bring forth; and that *thy blotts*
> And *mendings* tooke more time then *Fortune plot.*
> (*Jonsonus Virbius* 1638, 30)

Jonson, to some degree, defended himself against these charges: 'five weeks fully penn'd it,' he wrote of *Volpone*, 'From his owne hand, without a co-adiutor, / Novice, iourney-man, or tutor' ('Prologue,' Jonson 1937, 24); and he put the charge of fifteen weeks writing *Poetaster* into the mouth of Envy ('Induction,' Jonson 1932a, 203).[2] But he also, fundamentally, was committed to a culture of slow, laboured creativity. In his poem on Shakespeare that was printed in the 1623 First Folio, Jonson describes the process of writing poetry in terms of craft and work: he

> Who casts to write a living line, must sweat,
> (Such as thine are) and strike the second heat
> Upon the muses' anvil: turn the same,
> (And himself with it) that he thinks to frame;
> Or for the laurel, he may gain a scorn,
> For a good poet's made, as well as born.
> And such wert thou. (Jonson 1975, 265)

Shakespeare's lines endure because they are 'well-turned' and 'true-filed,' the product of hammer on anvil. This is the Jonson who began his professional life as a bricklayer, who 'wrought sometime,' according to Aubrey, 'with his father-in-lawe [a bricklayer], and particularly on the Garden-wall of Lincoln's-Inn next to Chancery-lane' (Aubrey 2000, 171). Jonson's discourse of creativity is powerfully shaped by a language of slow, meticulous production. 'A poem, as I have told you, is the work of the poet; the end and fruit of his labour and study. Poesy is his skill or craft of making' (*Discoveries*, Jonson 1975, 445).

Indeed, Jonson is sharply critical of hasty literary productivity. While post-Romantic culture tends to celebrate Shakespeare's suppos-

---

[2]   Jonson had a penchant for quantifying the dramatic experience: plays fill 'the space of two Hours and an half, and somewhat more' ('Induction,' *Bartholomew Fair*, Jonson 1938, 15); 'Fortune, that favours fools, these two short hours / We wish away' ('Prologue,' *The Alchemist*, Jonson 1937a, 294).

edly 'natural,' impulsive style, for Jonson this was Shakespeare's vice. 'I remember the players have often mentioned it as an honour to Shakspeare,' he wrote, 'that in his writing (whatsoever he penned) he never blotted out a line. My answer hath been, "Would he had blotted a thousand."' Jonson, who admired Shakespeare 'on this side [of] idolatry,' declared that an unchecked creativity was Shakespeare's principal fault: 'His wit was in his own power; would the rule of it had been so, too' (*Discoveries*, Jonson 1975, 394). If writing comes slowly, Jonson advised, 'cast not away the quills yet, nor scratch the wainscot, beat not the poor desk, but bring all to the forge and file again; torn it anew' (*Discoveries*, Jonson 1975, 447). The writer should punctuate periods of industry with sports and recreation, to grow 'stronger and more earnest by the ease' (*Discoveries*, Jonson 1975, 399). Pot-poets write quickly ('common rhymers pour forth verses'), but slow labour is a mark of good work. Jonson 'wrote all his first in prose, for so his master Camden, had learned him' Drummond noted (*Conversations*, Jonson 1975, 471), and 'if it comes in a year or two, it is well ... things wrote with labour deserve to be so read,' Jonson told himself in *Timber or Discoveries* (*Discoveries*, Jonson 1975, 448).

Good writing, according to Jonson, is the product of a lengthy process of reading the best authors, observing the best orators, and, crucially, gradually cultivating a literary style. The development of his style – what contemporary culture might call a 'voice' – comes, in Jonson's view, by practising, 'with diligence and often,' the 'placing and ranking [of] both matter and words.' This lengthy process of repetition 'quickens the heat of imagination,' and a sense of one's literary style as 'custom' or 'habit' gradually develops. One's 'natural' voice, in other words, is not natural at all, but the product of 'care and industry.' A poet does not 'leap forth suddenly ... by dreaming he hath ... washed his lips ... in Helicon' (*Discoveries*, Jonson 1975, 448).

In some ways it is helpful to conceive of Jonson's creativity – and of early modern creativity in general – as a process of organization; to think of *inventing* as *inventorying* what is already there. This was the period in which the commonplace book was the principal technology for retaining, organizing, and epitomizing a large body of information, and Jonson's reading and writing was shaped, to a considerable degree, by this textual form. The gathering, ordering, and subsequent deployment of quotations lay beneath much of Jonson's writing. In *Sejanus*, Jonson bolts down his sources through marginal references and cites, in his prefatory 'Letter To the Readers,' 'what Edition I follow'd. *Tacit. Lips.* in 4°, *Antuerp, edit.* 600; *Dio. Folio Hen. Step.* 92. For the rest, as

Sueton, Seneca, &c. the Chapter doth sufficiently direct, or the Edition is not varied' ('To the Readers,' Jonson 1932b, 351).

These quotations should normally, according to Jonson, be sufficiently digested so as to appear as the writer's own discourse; the good writer will 'be able to convert the substance or riches of another poet to his own use.' Jonson is explicit in identifying source passages in *Sejanus* in order to 'save myself in those common torturers that bring all wit to the rack.' But his overt citation of sources in this play indicates the degree to which his writing, in general, is informed by the organization of passages from classical texts.

Conclusion

Over the course of his career, Jonson frequently reflected on the nature of creativity. He did so by considering the scenes, objects, and habitual practices of writing, from the study to the tavern, and the pen to the seal. The ideal mode of creativity was the product of slow, careful, and industrious literary labour. That said, there is another side to Jonsonian creativity in which the heat of imagination is quickened not by the slow process of composition but through the fires of intoxication. The tensions between a convivial and conservative Jonson continue to structure his literary reputation.

In the early twentieth century, Alfred Noyes wrote his nostalgic *Tales of the Mermaid Tavern,* an extended dream-vision poem that begins by describing the speaker's meeting with Sir Walter Raleigh. Then the tavern begins to fill:

> There, flitting to and fro with cups of wine
> I heard them toss the Chrysomelan names
> From mouth to mouth – Lyly and Peele and Lodge,
> Kit Marlowe, Michael Drayton, and the rest,
> With Ben, rare Ben, brick-layer Ben, who rolled
> Like a great galleon on his ingle-bench. (Noyes 1913, 6)

The panel that once hung over the door to the Apollo Room, on which is written the verse welcoming 'all who lead or follow / To the oracle of Apollo,' survives, and can be found in the upstairs dining-room of the bank Child & Co. at 1 Fleet Street, London. The Apollo Room itself is long gone, disappearing with the Devil tavern in 1787 when Child took over the freehold and built his bank and a row of houses

(Jonson 1952, XI. 299). While Shakespeare is feted nightly in performances at the reconstructed Globe, just over the Thames, a convivial
Jonson continues to preside over the dining table.

Works Cited

Aubrey, John, 2000. *Brief Lives*, ed. Michael Hunter. London: Penguin.
Beaumont, Francis, 1660. *Poems. The Golden Remains of those so much admired
  Dramatick Poets, Francis Beaumont and John Fletcher*. London.
Boehrer, Bruce, 1997. *The Fury of Men's Gullets: Ben Jonson and the Digestive
  Canal*. Philadelphia: University of Pennsylvania Press.
Cave, Terence, 1985. *The Cornucopian Text: Problems of Writing in the French
  Renaissance*. 1979. Oxford: Oxford University Press.
Chamberlain, John, 1939. *The Letters of John Chamberlain*, ed. N. E. McClure.
  2 vols. Philadelphia: The American Philosophical Society.
Chartier, Roger, 1989. 'Leisure and Sociability: Reading Aloud in Early Modern
  Europe,' trans. Carol Mossman, in Susan Zimmerman and Ronald F. E.
  Weissman, eds, *Urban Life in the Renaissance*. Newark: University of Dela-
  ware Press.
Chartier, Roger, 2007. *Inscription and Erasure: Literature and Written Culture
  from the Eleventh to the Eighteenth Century*. Philadelphia: University of Penn-
  sylvania Press.
Clark, Peter, 1983. *The English Alehouse: A Social History, 1200–1830*. London:
  Longman.
Dekker, Thomas, 1970. *Satiromastix, or the untrussing of the Humorous Poet*,
  in *The Dramatic Works of Thomas Dekker*, I, ed. Fredson Bowers. 4 vols.
  Cambridge: Cambridge University Press.
Fuller, Thomas, 1662. *Histories*. London.
Herrick, Robert, 1921. *The Poetical Works*, ed. F. W. Moorman. London: Oxford
  University Press.
Howell, James, 1892. *Epistolae Ho-Elianae: The Familiar Letters of James Howell*,
  ed. J. Jacobs. 2 vols. London.
Jonson, Ben, 1927. *Every Man in His Humour*, in *Ben Jonson*, III, ed. C. H.
  Herford and Percy Simpson. 11 vols. Oxford: Clarendon Press.
Jonson, Ben, 1932a. *Poetaster*, in *Ben Jonson*, IV, ed. C. H. Herford and Percy
  Simpson. 11 vols. Oxford: Clarendon Press.
Jonson, Ben, 1932b. *Sejanus His Fall*, in *Ben Jonson*, IV, ed. C. H. Herford and
  Percy Simpson. 11 vols. Oxford: Clarendon Press.
Jonson, Ben, 1937a. *Alchemist*, in *Ben Jonson*, V, ed. C. H. Herford and Percy
  Simpson. 11 vols. Oxford: Clarendon Press.
Jonson, Ben, 1937b. *Volpone*, in *Ben Jonson*, V, ed. C. H. Herford and Percy
  Simpson. 11 vols. Oxford: Clarendon Press.
Jonson, Ben, 1938. *Bartholomew Fair*, in *Ben Jonson*, VI, ed. C. H. Herford and
  Percy Simpson. 11 vols. Oxford: Clarendon Press.

Jonson, Ben, 1952. *Ben Jonson*, XI, ed. C. H. Herford and Percy and Evelyn Simpson. 11 vols. Oxford: Clarendon Press.

Jonson, Ben, 1975. *The Complete Poems*, ed. George A. E. Parfitt. London: Penguin.

Jonsonus Virbius: or the Memorie of Ben Johnson Revived by the Friends of the Muses. 1638. London.

Kümin, Beat, and B. Ann Tlusty, eds, 2002. *The World of the Tavern*. Aldershot: Ashgate.

Loewenstein, Joseph, 2002. *Ben Jonson and Possessive Authorship*. Cambridge: Cambridge University Press.

Montaigne, Michel de, 1958. *The Complete Essays*, trans. and ed. Donald M. Frame. Stanford: Stanford University Press.

Nabbes, Thomas, 1637. *Hannibal and Scipio*. London.

Nochimson, Richard, 2002. '"Sharing" *The Changeling* by Playwrights and Professors: The Certainty of Uncertain Knowledge about Collaborations,' *Early Theatre*, 5 (1): 37–57.

Noyes, Alfred, 1913. *Tales of the Mermaid Tavern*. Blackwood: Edinburgh and London.

O'Callaghan, Michelle, 2007. *The English Wits: Literature and Sociability in Early Modern England*. Cambridge: Cambridge University Press.

Phillips, Edward, 1658. *The Mysteries of Love and Eloquence*. London.

Plutarch, 1969. *Moralia*, trans. Paul A. Clement and Herbert B. Hoffleit. Cambridge, MA: Harvard University Press.

Puttenham, George, 2007. *The Art of English Poesy. Contrived into Three Books (1589)*, ed. Frank Whigham and Wayne A. Rebhorn. Ithaca and London: Cornell University Press.

Sharpe, Kevin, 1979. *Sir Robert Cotton 1586–1631: History and Politics in Early Modern England*. Oxford: Oxford University Press.

Smyth, Adam, ed., 2004. *A Pleasing Sinne: Drink and Conviviality in Seventeenth-Century England*. Cambridge: D. S. Brewer.

Steggle, Matthew, 1999. 'Charles Chester and Ben Jonson,' *Studies in English Literature 1500–1900*, 39 (2): 313–26.

West, William, 2004. 'Reading Rooms: Architecture and Agency in the Houses of Michel de Montaigne and Nicholas Bacon,' *Comparative Literature*, 56 (2): 111–29.

Wit and Drollery, 1656.

Postscript

GRAEME HARPER

WHEN PASSING AN IDLE MOMENT perhaps consider: if H. G. Wells was a pacifist why did he play war strategy games with toy soldiers? Wells's life, and the period it was lived, is undoubtedly fascinating, so any brief contemplation will not be unpleasant, and certainly a valid enhancement of human knowledge should your location in academe require you to confirm you are not idling without intent. And, indeed, it is not an illogical scholarly contemplation either: not only did Wells enjoy playing with toy soldiers, he wrote books to explore this play. Thus, primary textual evidence! In *Floor Games* (1911) Wells considers the theory and method of playing children's games involving models and miniatures, while in *Little Wars* (1913) he goes further in offering a set of rules for playing with toy soldiers, as well as a high degree of personal emotional enthusiasm to accompany those rules.

It is entirely possible, from your contemplation, and informed by a range of material evidence, to construct a biography of this toy-soldiering Wells, relating his interests to his finished works, and exploring his varied relationships with war and propaganda, Socialism, science, teaching, haberdashery, sketching, the machinations of Modernity, and marriage and/or relationships (if you might bravely follow that fascinating labyrinth). Indeed, Herbert George Wells can be deservingly encapsulated. Though, if you do so, are you not already building another-Wells? Might this creature in our biographical sights be more akin, that is, to your-Wells? Their-Wells? Our-Wells? Her-Wells? His-Wells? Or not Wells at all? Might it be more akin to Shelley's Frankenstein? This is not criticism of biography. It is not pointing out the follies of engaging in literary criticism. In some ways, in fact, it is a plea for the creativity embodied in critical reflection on finished works of Literature and the writers of these. It is however, more significantly, a question, when considering creative writers and creative writing, about where it is most appropriate to begin.

When discussing 'Creative Environments' we cannot do anything other than ask ourselves about the human actions that might be occurring within these environments. Unless, of course, we're talking about the creative lives of bees or bears, seals or swallows – which, of course, in the case of creative writing, we're obviously not. Human actions, human understandings, human time, and human place: these are the things we're exploring in considering 'Creative Environments.'

Enter, then, the biographically reconstructed Wells; textually represented Wells; accessed, appreciated, appreciable Wells. A subject of analysis, he has all the attributes of being a human being. And, depicted in a combination of biographical observation and textual investigation, he certainly looks the part. Dressed up like this, he can contribute to discussions of such things as sexual freedom, German militarism or the European Union. He represents *fin de siècle* evidential weight very well too; he is, after all, not a creative writer obscured by lack of fame; a foreign language (here in largely English-speaking Britain); a penchant for destroying evidence of his creations; a tendency towards ferocious privacy; or by the will of relatives who have sought to remake him. Nor is this Wells hidden by the obscurity of his completed works; or by the simple manipulation of that thing we are inclined to call History.

Were we avid E. H. Carr fans, perhaps poring over *What is History?* (Carr 1985) in another moment of contemplation, we would recognize that our Wells, my-Wells, your-Wells is, in fact, not only unobscured by History but positively enhanced by it. Not to say that Carr argues for the primacy of interpretation over facts. Nor does he argue for the insurmountable wonder of facts over interpretation. Rather, he suggests that historiography that is too enamoured of factual investigation becomes mere antiquarianism, a 'fetishism of facts' (Carr 1985, 16). Alternatively, historiography that is overwhelmed by interpretation has no chance of approaching Truth. History, Carr says, is in reality 'an unending dialogue between the present and the past' (30).

Naturally therefore, if we write good History, Wells changes – but, in truth, not in the way that Wells himself changed. And Wells did change. He changed within, and because of, his creative environment. He constructed it, reacted to it, and he recreated it. Wells the pacifist appears not to be Wells the eugenicist. Nor, indeed, does Wells the socialist look much like Wells the diabetic; nor Wells the teacher act much like Wells the artist. Alternatively, of course, he was all these things, and more.

Much as science in the later nineteenth and twentieth centuries increasingly came to be associated with social complexity, so the history of the writer Herbert George Wells reveals a complexity layered with disposition, cultural norms, artistic intentions, political rules, social constructs, numerous emotions, economic necessities, group goals, and

individual reasons. But by each insistence we make on the combination
of fact and interpretation that builds our nicely reconstructed Wells,
we construct a Wells whose relationship with his creative environment is, at best, an amalgam, and not an entirety. Approach such a
reconstruction holistically and the analysis is likely to fail to highlight
important substance, because the sheer number of facts overwhelms
interpretation; approach this from an individualist perspective, based
on Wells's importance as a creative writer, and interpretation inevitably
overcomes facts: and we, thus, fail to produce truth.

It is striking to use Wells to make this point. Not only does the
period in which he wrote lend itself to explorations of what is perhaps
not so much the turmoil of a new era as the vibrancy of a new inter-
connectedness. It also asks us to consider the relationship between the
individual and the society – in essence, the indivisibility of this relationship.

Wells's creative environment is, simplistically, indivisible from the
self and from the cultural milieu in which he found himself. But behind
this truism lies something less discussed and more significant. That
is: the nature and style of that environmental exchange. We could –
perhaps taking us back to those bees, bears, and swallows – we could
talk in terms of *habitat*. But how comfortable would a literary critic be
in doing so? Do we feel empowered, for example, to talk of the habitats
of poets or the habitats of novelists? A habitat can refer to an ecological
community or to a controlled environment. So, is there an ecology
of poetic environments? Can we manufacture and control a novelistic
habitat?

These questions bring us, in the contemporary academic world, to
that significant discussion of whether creative writing can be taught.
Creative Writing – a subject that has a close association with English,
along with its other associations with such academic subjects as
Drama, Film and Media, Music, and Education – Creative Writing
has often been questioned as an academic subject on the grounds that
constructing, or indeed reconstructing, the actual experiences of creative writers is an impossibility. That the notion of providing a useful
creative writing habitat in higher education is a falsehood and, at best,
that we can merely encourage or direct, but never provide an environment that can truly allow us to teach creative writers. Again, returning
to the case of H. G. Wells helps us with this debate.

The solution to the problem of discussing the creative environments
of creative writers is revealed, on the basis of the Wellsian example, to

be this: take a creative writer who has a penchant for war games using toy soldiers. Imagine him in a period in which wars occur. Consider the reasons, nature, and form or these wars, and the reasons, nature, and form of the war games he plays. Include in this consideration any textual evidence. See him within an entire *fin de siècle* habitat, both micro (his home, for example, and evidence of his interests, relationships, thoughts) and macro (the world around him, society, the political and economic milieu). Acknowledge he has a personality, a disposition, a will, emotions, intentions. Imagine him, to choose a seemingly pure material artefact, in a period in which the telephone was invented. This is not a random technological reference! Today we see the telephone, in its mobile form, changing our relationship with time and space. We phone in motion; we bridge time zones while moving through space. The mobile phone is, in some ways, the closest thing to time travel so far invented. For Wells, whether we have demonstrative textual evidence of this or not, such a technology, even in its earliest form, must have at very least piqued his interest. This, we interpret.

We interpret, as Carr would suggest, not only on the basis of found facts but on the basis of our own historical location – simply, our mobile phone becomes Wells's telephone. Naturally, then, *our* Wells cannot be *the* Wells. He is *a* Wells. But, in order for him to be any true Wells whatsoever, we must envisage his creative environment as both ecological and manufactured; factual evidence and our interpretative strengths must balance. If we refer to another general definition of habitat, Wells's creative environment, if we are to consider it, and perhaps understand it, needs to be *the place he is most likely to be found*. In this albeit reconstructed environment, the existence of works such as *Floor Games* and *Little Wars* begins to make more sense. The relationship between these texts and Wells's personal life becomes clearer; as does the nature of an individual psychology and physiology that engages in toy soldiering. Our response to, and virtual reconstruction of, the environment in which these works were written also captures such other works as *The Time Machine* (1895) and *The Island of Dr Moreau* (1896).

So *The Time Machine* sits well alongside Nobel Laureate Henri Bergson's *Matter and Memory* (1896) as a text indicative of ideas prevalent in the macro environment of the *fin de siècle*, yet demonstrating the micro environment in which Wells the creative writer responded, made creative choices, articulated his emotions, composed and acted upon his intentions and reasons. Both texts look at the temporal distinctions between body and spirit rather than the Cartesian spatial distinctions, yet both *belong* not merely to a culture but also to individual writers. And these creative writers engaged with their creative environments fluidly, in personal and public acts, through thoughts and feelings. Simply considering textual evidence cannot get us close to the truth of their habitats.

Similarly, with its explorations of nature versus nurture, *The Island of Dr Moreau* rather neatly takes us back to the question of how environments shape organisms, but it also reminds us that we are dealing with ethnographic materials, phenomena not mere materials. It is for this reason, though here is not the place to debate it, that creative writing can be taught – because creative writing is not determined by texts; rather it is determined, and propelled, by humans and human phenomena.

There is probably no better place to stop, or start, our contemplation than this. Because it is in the engagement with the human action of creative writing, and in incorporating textual evidence of that action into a wider, and deeper, consideration of the phenomenon of human creativity, that we begin to understand and articulate the nature of creative environments. In doing so, we get closer to the truth of writerly production while recognizing that in each meld of fact and interpretation we reveal as much about ourselves as we do about the creative writer. Today's interconnected, mobile world must surely assist us in progressing these investigations.

Works Cited

Carr, E. H., 1985. *What is History?* Harmondsworth: Penguin (orig. published 1961).

Index

archives and libraries, 8–10, 73, 69–77, 103–4, 156–8
Auden, W.H., 10, 21–38
authenticity, 149–50

de Balzac, Honoré, 22
Beckett, Samuel, 22–3, 47
Bilton, Christopher, 5–6, 8
Brontë family, 107–24
Burns, Robert, 12

cento, 44
Clare, John, 10
Coleridge, Samuel Taylor, 21–2
copyright and plagiarism, 75–6, 159
creative education, 6–8, 10–11, 29, 47–8, 103, 105, 151, 152, 175
creative industries, 5–6, 7–8, 125–8
creative process, 2–4, 10, 12–14, 42–4, 31–3, 50, 66–7, 76, 94–8, 105, 115–17

data protection, 75–6
Dickens, Charles, 10, 62, 63, 91
Donne, John, 10

Eliot, George, 51, 58, 65, 89
English Subject Centre, 11
e-texts, 9, 69, 101–5

Florida, Richard, 4–5
forgery 10
Fortey, Richard, 43–4
Freud, Sigmund, 3

Gaskell, Elizabeth, 52, 65, 113, 115, 122
gender, 50–3, 59, 109–10, 116, 142–3
government funding, 7, 70, 76, 149, 152

Hall, John, 105

handwriting, 83, 93, 112–13
Hazlitt, William, 44
Heartfield, James, 8
heritage industry, 65–6, 72–4, 76, 92, 107–8, 134, 147–54
Hollinghurst, Alan, 44–5
Houseman, A.E., 12

Isherwood, Christopher, 27, 28–9

James, Henry, 59, 65
Johnson, Samuel, 10
Jonson, Ben, 155–72

Kallman, Chester, 24, 26, 27–8, 33, 37
knowledge economy, 8

Landry, Charles, 4–5
Larkin, Philip, 9, 10, 41, 47, 71
Levinas, Emmanuel, 103
literary festivals, 125–8
Logue, Christopher, 21

manuscript, 69–71, 74–5, 107, 109, 115, 138
MacNeice, Louis, 32
Maslow, Abraham, 4
Milton, John, 129–46
de Montaigne, Michel, 156
Motion, Andrew, 9, 39–48

Norse, Harold, 23–5, 26

Oliphant, Margaret, 97, 49–68
Olivier, Richard, 7
Open University, The, 6–7
Owen, Wilfred, 46

Patterson, Don, 105
Pinter, Harold, 72–3, 76
Poe, Edgar Allan, 12
Poincaré, Henri, 2

Pound, Ezra, 18
publishers, 25–7, 58, 59, 63–5, 84, 88

de Quincey, Thomas, 10

rhetoric, 11
Ritchie, Anne Thackeray, 53

Shakespeare, William, 46, 73, 77,
    147–54
Spender, Stephen, 25, 31–2, 37

Thackeray, 91
Tennyson, Alfred, 51
Thomas, Edward, 44, 46
Trollope, Anthony, 79–100

Wallas, Graham, 2, 3
Wells, H.G., 173–7
Wesley, John, 10
Winkworth, Catherine, 113–14
Winnicott, D.W., 3
Woolf, Virginia, 97
Wordsworth, William, 12, 21, 44, 46
work habits:
    alcohol and drugs, 34, 50–1, 160–6
    amanuenses, 93, 131–2, 139, 142
    ambition, 129–31

collaboration, 27–9, 156–9
craftsmanship, 166–9
daydreaming, vision, and trance,
    50, 51, 94–5, 115–17, 118–19
extemporization, 161–2
friends and families, 28–9, 44–5,
    46–7, 56–7, 122, 157–8
hours, 33–4, 37, 39–40, 42, 59–61,
    64, 85–7, 89, 93, 131
income from writing, 50, 51–2, 91
jobs, other, 50, 64–5, 79–88, 91–2
letter and life-writing, 120–2
sight and blindness, 117–19, 133–4,
    135, 136–8
place, 1, 2, 4–5, 21–5, 31–7,
    42, 52–6, 59, 61, 85, 107–8,
    111–14, 119, 122, 134–5, 150–1,
    156–7, 175–7
play 3, 107–8, 109–11, 114–15,
    125–6, 173
reception, 64, 97, 104–5
revision, 22, 26, 29, 44, 62–4, 83–4,
    168
writer's block, 39–41, 47, 85–6,
    93–4

Yonge, Charlotte, 52